A COURSE IN MIRACLES AND. . .

A Course in Miracles and...

Christian, Jew, Muslim, shaman, Zoroastrian,
stone, ground, mountain, river,
each has a secret way of being with the mystery,
unique and not to be judged.
Sufi Mystic Rumi (1213-1273)

Compiled, written and edited by
Jon Mundy, Ph.D. & Lorri Coburn, M.S.W.

COGENT
PUBLISHING NY
IMPRINT OF
THE WHITSON GROUP, INC.

Published by Cogent Publishing NY
Imprint of The Whitson Group, Inc.
3 Miller Road, Putnam Valley, NY 10579
(845) 528-7617 • www.cogentpub.com
cogentpub@aol.com

Front cover designed by Brad Oliphant, Fine Art Photography NY.
www.bradoliphantphotography.com

ISBN: 978-0-925776-45-7
1 2 3 4 5—19 18 17

Are other teachers possible, to lead the way
to those who speak in different tongues
and appeal to different symbols?
Certainly there are.
Would God leave anyone without
a very present help in time of trouble;
a savior who can symbolize Himself?

A COURSE IN MIRACLES (M-23.7:2-4)

Table of Contents

Introduction

Are other teachers possible, to lead the way to those who speak in different tongues and appeal to different symbols? Certainly there are.

> *Would God leave anyone without a very present help in time of trouble; a savior who can symbolize Himself?*
>
> **A Course in Miracles (M-23.7:2-4)**

Reading the teachings of the world's great scriptural traditions and knowing the wisdom of *A Course in Miracles*, an inevitable conversation takes place regarding the similarities and differences between the teaching of the Course and a host of different mystics, philosophers, and spiritual teachings. Spend time reading the Course and you'll soon say. "Who wrote this?" It is soon clear that no "body" wrote it. It's a most amazing document. Perhaps "the" most incredible document ever to cross the face of planet earth. Nothing is more fascinating than an exploration of the divine and everyone wants to know what happens when we leave our bodies behind forever.

It is the intention of this book to show how many of the ideas contained in *A Course in Miracles* are reflected in a host of different religions, individual thinkers and schools of thought which both pre-dated the printing of the Course and can now be found in the teaching of other contemporary teachings.

> *The truth is true.*
> *Nothing else matters, nothing else is real,*
> *and everything beside it is not there.*
>
> **T-14.II.3:3-4**

Innumerable truth seekers, mystics, philosophers, and just regular folks, even children, have had insights into the nature of reality and they have been able to tell us about it. I was watching a 15 year-old girl on television talking about her near death experience and she kept saying, "everything is all connected." She said it over and again in amazement.

The concept of non-dualism, that is, a teaching that God is God or Truth is True and there can be no opposite, is basic to the earliest spiritual teachings. It can be found in Advaita Vedanta, which traces its roots back to the *Upanishads*, the world's oldest scriptures. Much of the truth we find in the Course can also be found in the Bhagavad Gita, the teachings of Judaism, Zen Buddhism, Sufism, the teaching of Jesus in the New Testament, the Quakers, Christian Science, Unity, Science of Mind, Alcoholics Anonymous, Gestalt Psychology, and the teachings of a host of individual teachers like: Rudolf Steiner, Edgar Cayce, Jiddu Krishnamurti, and David Hawkins, to name a few. The list goes on.

This is an anthology—a collection of selected works by a host of different writers each previously published in earlier editions of Miracles magazine. I've been slowly putting this book together for over 15 years. Then, an angel in the form of Lorri Coburn came along and said, "When are you ever going to finish that book, people want to see it." To which I responded, "Why don't you help me?" And, she did, by editing the entire book, by writing two of the chapters herself and by contacting and securing permission for inclusion of each of the chapters by the various writers whose names appear inside.

This book might be Volume 1. There may be another edition or several editions which show further overlaps, similarities and differences between the Course and a host of other teachings on the nature of reality. Though we have a chapter on Sufism, I would love to see a chapter on traditional Islam, as well as chapters on other schools of thought and teachers from the past like the Gnostics, Neo-Platonism, Carl Jung, Joel Goldsmith, Carlos Castaneda and Osho as well as current teachers like Eckhart Tolle, Richard Bach, Ken Wilbur, Byron Katie, Matthew Fox, Mooji, Richard Rohr, and more. We'll keep running such articles in Miracles magazine and see how this develops. If you have an idea for another comparison or you would like to write a chapter yourself, let me know. Jon@miraclesmagazine.org.

As this is a collection of writing by a host of writers, we should note at the outset that, the views and opinions of individual authors are not necessarily those of the editors. For some spiritual paths, we have included more than one article, as they highlight different aspects of *A Course in Miracles*.

Referencing *A Course in Miracles*

In "A Course in Miracles and..." all quotes from the Course italicized.

A Course in Miracles is divided into several sections—Text, Workbook for Students, Manual for Teachers, Clarification of Terms, plus supplements—Psychotherapy: Purpose, Process and Practice, and The Song of Prayer. The reference for each quote or paraphrase appears immediately after the quote, listing the chapter, section, paragraph, and sentence For example, T-9.III.4:1 references Text-chapter 9.section III.paragraph 4:sentence 1; W-pI.67.6:2 references Workbook-partI. lesson 67.paragraph 6:sentence.

T references *Text*
W references *Workbook*
M references *Manual for Teachers*
p references Part I or II of *Workbook*
C references *Clarification of Terms*
P references *Psychotherapy: Purpose, Process, and Practice*
S references *The Song of Prayer*
in references *Introduction*
R references *Review*
Ep references Epilogue

In this book, *A Course in Miracles* is generally referred to simply as "the Course." Sometimes lines from the Course are in ***bold*** for emphasis. Only rarely does the Course itself boldface a word or phrase within a sentence. However, there are many words and phrases that the Course italicizes for emphasis.

Section I

Eastern Religious Teachings

Chapter 1

Hawaiian Spirituality

Constance Stevens

It may seem like a real stretch to think about finding similarities between *A Course in Miracles* and indigenous Hawaiian spirituality. Lovely as the words and images are in the Text and Workbook, *A Course in Miracles'* language hardly conjures sensual images of beautiful sun-kissed Hawaiians laying bouquets of lush tropical flowers on a steaming volcano floor. However, western civilization's understanding of Hawaiian spirituality has been severely misguided ever since 1820 when Christian missionaries first made contact with Hawaiian natives. The missionaries gathered their information from Hawaiian farmers, fishermen, and craftspersons, who knew nothing of the esoteric teachings of the *kahuna* (spiritual leaders).

The oral tradition teachings of the kahuna were mystified further when they were outlawed and forced into secrecy beginning only 11 years after the missionaries' arrival. Although some Hawaiian ritualistic practices were decriminalized in 1919, anything considered "sorcery" was illegal until 1972. To this secrecy, add the drama of stories describing human sacrifice and even mistaken rumors of cannibalism, and you have a spiritual world that seems to be at the extreme opposite to *A Course in Miracles.*

Not so.

According to Ku, Kahuna Lokahi, Hawaiian spirituality is based on understanding three things. *First*, we are divine beings. As divine beings, we create the world around us. *Second*, there is no duality. All is One, and we are still One with God. There is no fallen state of sin. *Third*, errors in perception cause unhappy memories that are the source of all suffering. Hawaiian practice emphasizes living in the present, forgiving ourselves and others, doing no harm, acting from our hearts, and living without judgment of others.

Sound familiar? Hawaiian spirituality is so radical in its deepest teachings that it is surprisingly comparable to *A Course in Miracles.*

There are differences in form and imagery that hide the similarity of content. Hawaiians deliberately live in harmony with the earth and greatly value family and ancestors. They acknowledge an energetic substance connecting all things called "aka," and a life force called "mana." There are beings on the other side of death who are honored as deities or as older brothers and sisters, who remain close to the living and sometimes interact with daily life. Hawaiians live both in the visible physical world and the invisible world of spirit and energy.

However, in essence, Hawaiian spirituality is very much like *A Course in Miracles*. It seeks to reveal the true identity of man. This identity is discovered by recognizing the spiritual part of ourselves that connects to the Universal Spirit of God. Kaula Laura Kealoha Yardley, Ph.D., teaches that we go within ourselves and find the voice that will answer our questions and lead us to the light. The voice leads us to discover that we *are* the Universal Mind or Spirit! We find God within, because Spirit is One and we are all part of the One.

The Course describes this same experience. It states that there is a Voice for God, the Holy Spirit, which is found inside every person and always leads to Oneness with God:

> *This is the Voice for God, reminding you of your Father and of your Self. This is the Voice of truth, replacing everything that the ego tells you about yourself with the simple truth about the Son of God.*
>
> W-PI.67.6:2-3

The Three Selves and the Ego

The Hawaiians know that a person is more than a just a body. Hawaiian spiritual practice is based on an understanding of human consciousness: its nature, dimensions and divisions, as well as the forces through which the elements of consciousness work. Its psychologically sophisticated paradigm has remarkable similarities to *A Course in Miracles*.

Non-native Hawaiian researcher, Max Freedom Long, who founded the Huna Fellowship in 1945, noted that few in the West knew of the unconscious until Freud. Yet, he maintained, the kahuna of ancient Hawaii knew not only of its existence, but also of its special and important functions. This is evident in the Hawaiian concept of the person, which recognizes three separate but interacting selves: (1) the lower self (Unihipili), (2) the middle self (Uhane), and (3) the higher Self (Aumakua).

The lower self (Unihipili): This is the body, the emotions, the subconscious, and the inner self where memory resides. From this perspective we see only the past, and we experience feelings of sin, guilt and fear.

Kahuna David Kaonohiokala Bray, Sr., explained that in the lower self level, we create unreality through misperception and misinterpretation, which lead to negative emotions and wrong actions, and these in turn lead to unhappiness, illness, and death. Most of humanity is caught in the illusory trap that consciousness is centered in the body, with perhaps flashes of insight into the soul level. From this body level, we view our relation to God as servitude. We perceive through senses limited in time and space, conditioned by the past (memory) and the future (anticipation), and the result is egoism, frustration, and the experience of pleasure and pain. This bodily consciousness is based on a perceived separation or division of subject and object, as between ourselves and others.

In *A Course in Miracles*, this *lower self* is the ego in the body, the embodiment of the illusion of separation.

The middle self (Uhane): This is the conscious self, which has full reasoning power, will power and imagination, but no memory (no perception of the past). Only the middle self can sin, and the only sin is to hurt another person willfully. The middle self, the intellect, cannot solve problems, because its function is only to manage.

A person's goal as a conscious middle self is to learn about, establish contact with, and work harmoniously with the low self and the high self. The union of three selves creates harmony and balance. Union is achieved by forgiving others, for as long as we are blocked in our middle self by holding a grudge or hating someone, the low self will not be able to get through to the higher Self.

Everything begins in the middle self because it is the mind. Until one has conceived of something in the mind, one is unable to project that thought or a manifestation of that thought out into the world. In *A Course in Miracles*, this *middle self* aspect is the decision-maker, the part of us who knows it can choose another way.

The higher Self (Aumakua): The higher Self or Aumakua is the god-self. The Aumakua knows intuitively, and can be in contact with the higher powers of Spirit as well as with other peoples' higher Selves, known as the *Great Company of Higher Selves.*

A Course in Miracles has a similar concept referred to as the Self, which cannot be separated from the Creator. Like the Aumakua in contact with the Great Company of Higher Selves, the Self of *A Course in Miracles* is part of the greater Sonship (T-7.IX.2:1-2).

Healing

Healing is getting rid of guilt, through the process of going back and undoing the hurt. Healing is really a process of giving up the ego. All healing, in the kahuna view, is the result of a natural communion with the Aumakua (the higher Self), allowing its Divine Source energy to flow freely along the original pattern of perfection. All illness or distortion of any kind results from interference with that flow. The most direct healing of body, mind, and circumstance comes through consciously involving the Aumakua in one's thoughts, emotions, and daily life in an open, loving, and trusting way. Healing is accomplished as the lower and middle selves harmonize with the higher Self, the Great Company of Higher Selves, and the divine.

Similarly, *A Course in Miracles* teaches that we are healed as we release our grievances and our error of perceived separation from God and from the rest of the Sonship, stating, *"healing always produces harmony, because it proceeds from integration"* (T-7.V.6:6).

Forgiveness and Ho'oponopono

A Course in Miracles teaches that forgiveness is recognizing the unaltered divine perfection in our brothers and our sisters as well as in ourselves.

> *Forgiveness recognizes what you thought your brother did to you has not occurred. It does not pardon sins and make*

them real. It sees there was no sin. And in that view are all your sins forgiven. What is sin, except a false idea about God's Son? Forgiveness merely sees its falsity, and therefore lets it go.

W-pII.1.1:1-6

Hawaiian ho'oponopono is different. It is the practice of restoring harmonious flow and balance among people. In ho'oponopono, not only does the individual forgive the other for the creation of error and disharmony, but the individual also assumes responsibility for all error and requests forgiveness. There is a practical reason for accepting this complete responsibility, which is also recognized in *A Course in Miracles.* While we can forgive the other person, we cannot change the other person. The only thing we can change is our own mind. This is how all judgment of the other is released, through accepting responsibility and changing our own mind. This practice is based on the truth that there is nothing separate from ourselves, so there is nothing that is not us and cannot be changed, if we change ourselves.

Kahuna Morrnah Nalamaku Simeona, in using an updated form of ho'oponopono, explains that we are the sum total of our experiences, which is to say that we are burdened by our pasts. When we experience stress or fear in our lives, we find that the cause is actually a memory. It is the emotions tied to the memory that affect us in the present. The subconscious always associates an action or person in the present with something that happened in the past. When this occurs, emotions are activated and stress is produced.

This is quite similar to some of the first lessons in *A Course in Miracles*, including, "*I see only the past,*" and "*What I see is a form of vengeance*" (W-pI.7.h; 22.h).

Kahuna Morrnah teaches that the main purpose of this process of ho'oponopono is to discover Divinity within oneself. Ho'oponopono is a profound gift which allows one to develop a working relationship with the Divinity within, and to learn to ask that in each moment, our errors in thought, word, deed, or action be cleansed through forgiveness. Because we are One with all Being, Kahuna Morrnah uses the following liturgy: "Divine creator, father, mother, son as One...If I, my family, relatives and ancestors have offended you, your family, relatives or ancestors in thoughts, words, deeds and actions from the beginning of our creation to the present, we ask forgiveness...Let this cleanse, purify, release, cure all the negative memories, blocks, energies and vibrations and transmute these unwanted energies to pure light... And it is done."

Therapist Ihaleakala Hew Len, Ph.D., also teaches that everything you seek and everything you experience exists inside you, because all is One and there is no separation. Because you create everything in your life, it follows that you have created all problems you discover—even a client's or friend's problems or problems you read about or see on television. There is no one to blame for anything; the responsibility is entirely your own. If you want to change anything, you must change it on the inside, not the outside. You clear your own mind through forgiveness.

One of the methods Dr. Hew Len uses for such cleansing forgiveness is by silently stating to one's own self, an aggrieved other person, and/or to the Divine Source, "I am sorry. Please forgive me. I love you. Thank you." Repeating this clears away the error *inside* the speaker, and in changing the speaker, changes the non-separated other person or circumstance. It is important to understand that Dr. Hew Len's technique, stating, "I am sorry; Please forgive me," is meant to accept responsibility for the problem, and not to encourage feelings of personal guilt. As in *A Course in Miracles*, the kahunas teach that guilt and the ego must be transcended.

The Vision

The kahuna of Hawaii believe that you do not have to go anywhere else or do anything different in order to become enlightened. The vast reaches of the soul, the universal mind, the divine, are always available to each of us. To find this one only needs to turn inside, because the source of the infinite is always there waiting for us. This core truth is in perfect accord with the teachings of *A Course in Miracles.*

Constance Stevens is a retired attorney and former law school professor. She is an initiated kahuna in a branch of the Ku lineage, and a healer in the Hawaiian tradition. Connie is a practitioner of Reconnective Healing and of The Reconnection. She is also a certified Bio-energy Field Transmitter, and a photographer of orbs and mystical light images. *A Course in Miracles* has been her spiritual practice since 1986.

Chapter 2

The Bhagavad Gita

Arvind Kumar

The *Bhagavad Gita* (these Sanskrit words can be translated as "The Song Divine") is perhaps the most widely known and read of the Hindu scriptures. Written around two-thousand years ago in Sanskrit, the *Bhagavad Gita* (referred to as simply the *Gita* by many) has been translated into most languages spoken in the world today.

There are numerous commentaries available on the *Gita*. Many well-known recent, as well as ancient, personalities have commented upon their experience of getting to know the *Gita* as one of the most mind-transforming scriptures. These include: Albert Einstein, Mahatma Gandhi, Dr. Albert Schweitzer, Sri Aurobindo, Carl Jung, India's Prime Minister Nehru, Herman Hesse, Vivekananda, Ralph Waldo Emerson, Paramahansa Yogananda, Rudolph Steiner, Adi Shankara, Aldous Huxley, Ramana Maharshi and Nisargadatta Maharaj. The *Gita* is considered one of the greatest spiritual books ever written. It was a most wonderful experience for me to read several commentaries on it, and I liked the *Gita* so much that at the age of 50, I was able to commit to memory some 150 verses (out of a total of 700) in the original Sanskrit, even though my knowledge of Sanskrit is most rudimentary.

I was born in 1951 in India to a Hindu family and over the years have had the good fortune of being exposed to various Indian scriptures known as *Upanishads,* which comprise what is commonly called *Vedanta* (a Sanskrit term meaning "the end of the Vedas," or "the highest knowledge"). I came to North America in 1975, and after getting married and settling down here, I began my spiritual quest in earnest. As part of that quest, I studied the *Vedas* and the various *Upanishads* over a period of several years and found that there was general, though not universal, agreement that the *Bhagavad Gita* represents the essence of all Hindu scripture.

I was introduced to *A Course in Miracles* in April 2002 and was immediately struck by its similarity to *Advaita Vedanta*, which was also commented upon by Bill Thetford in an interview he gave in October 1984 to *New Realities* magazine. (See www.miraclestudies.net/BillInterv.html).

I am by no means an expert on either the Course or the *Gita*, but I have been an earnest student of both, with the Course being my primary focus and spiritual path. The purpose of this discussion includes the following:

1. To understand that a central theme in both of these scriptures is that truth is one, paths are many, and as the Course says:

   > *A universal theology is impossible, but a universal experience is not only possible but necessary. It is this experience toward which the Course is directed. Here alone consistency becomes possible because here alone uncertainty ends.*
   >
   > C-IN.2:5-7

2. To increase our commitment to awakening from the dream life of this physical world, which is the common message of both of these scriptures.
3. To increase our devotion to the Course as our path as we verify its commonality with a widely regarded, valid ancient scripture to liberation. By the same token, if the Gita is our path, to increase our devotion to the *Gita*, as its message is verified by a relatively modern scripture. It is certainly not necessary for Course students or for *Gita* students to run to other scriptures, as that could delay their awakening. The emphasis in both scriptures is on *practice*, and the Course as well as the *Gita* each give us all that we need to practice in order to awaken from our dream. In my case, the *Gita* was the first scripture I read but when I read the Course, I got additional insights into what the *Gita* was pointing to! Many others have reported a similar experience, and perhaps it will pay interested readers to study both scriptures, if they are so guided.

How the Course Builds on the *Gita*

There is perhaps no modern teaching that emphasizes *innocence* and *unity* in more straightforward terms than the Course. There seems to be no other teaching besides the Course that ranks itself more clearly as just one of many, as a temporary aid only, and as helpful to some but not to all. The Course does not present itself as superior to other authentic teachings on the subject of awakening. Many of these ideas are present in the *Gita* as well, and it is possible, indeed inevitable, for students of the Course to gain significantly by a dedicated study of the *Gita*, for truth needs to be heard in many different ways, again and again, in the pursuit of awakening.

What can be considered as common between the two scriptures includes the following:

1. The origin of the scripture—*apaurusheya* or non-human, heard by human beings in their state of right-mindedness, by connecting with Jesus in the case of the Course, and Krishna in the case of the *Bhagavad Gita* (which forms a small part of the *Mahabharata*, with origin rooted in deep mystery
2. What triggered these scriptures?—a question on the part of those engaged in the battleground of this world. In the Gita, the mighty warrior, Arjuna, was confused as to whether he should fight or not, on seeing people he respected arrayed against him on the opposite side in battle. For the Course, two professors in the Columbia Presbyterian School of Medical Psychology asked to see another way to deal with their constant relationship struggle;
3. A unique Guru-disciple relationship—the scripture is transmitted in a one-on-one setting, but its message is universal, for entire humanity;
4. Demonstrations in the lives of the respective teachers—Jesus in the Course, and Krishna in the *Gita*. This illustrates the principle that true scripture is not what is written on paper but rather is exemplified through the seeming life of the teacher. Likewise, the means for human beings to be true followers of scripture is not its intellectual understanding but rather, the requirement of *living* the teaching;
5. Masterpieces of art—poetic, symphonic, and holographic characteristics.

I do not see any conflict between the *Gita* and the Course as far as their basic message is concerned. There are several areas where they complement each other nicely. The "extra" benefits and insights I gathered upon reading the Course include:

* First-hand description in English (as opposed to translations from the original Sanskrit) of a very comforting but non-compromising non-dual thought system, with additional details on the state of Heaven, knowledge, and creation to contrast it with the world of perception.
* A detailed description of the seeming split from the perfection of Godhead into the world out here, with the concomitant arising of sin, guilt, fear, and chaos that human beings face. (That is, we created the world as an attack on God, an attack so carefully crafted that we actually forgot we did it. Thus, we could not go back to undo it very easily; it is a mad dream that we could actually hide from God.)
* A detailed explanation that the world I see with the body's eyes is an effect of my split mind. A part of my mind bought into the idea that separation from God is possible; and as such, projected an illusory world. I am completely responsible for everything I see, and squarely in charge of salvation of the world.
* A very detailed exposition of our *special relationships* which are the crown jewels in the ego's strategy to keep us separate as individuals in this world.
* The use of the body and the world as a classroom for learning the lessons of forgiveness, which paves the way back to the world of spirit.

Essence of the Gita

How to live life in this world, a life so transient and apparently full of sorrows? What is the abiding Truth sought by man throughout the ages? In answer to these questions, Krishna offered the eternal message of wisdom, "know thyself," which is the quintessence of the Course and every authentic spiritual tradition. Bhagavan Sri Ramana Maharshi, at the request of devotees, selected forty-two of the seven-hundred verses of the *Bhagavad Gita*, and arranged them in a particular order, which can be found in the booklet *Song Celestial.* These forty-two verses contain the essence of the *Bhagavad Gita*, and they show the aspirant the direct means to realize the Self Absolute, which is the one, ultimate object of man's quest throughout the ages. Here are a few of these verses:

The Blessed Lord said:

> 10.20 I am the Self, O Arjuna, dwelling in the Heart of every being; I am the beginning and the middle, and likewise the end of all beings.
>
> 4.19 Whose every enterprise is without desire or motive, whose actions are burnt up in the fire of knowledge, him the wise call a Sage.
>
> 2.71 Having cast away all desires, that man who goes without longing, devoid of *I* and *mine*—he doth attain peace.
>
> 18.62 Unto Him alone surrender, O Arjuna, with all thy being; by His Grace shalt thou obtain Peace Supreme, the Abode Eternal.
>
> 11:54 To seek the Self and abide as one with it in the Heart is at once the path of knowledge and devotion. In that state there is no *otherness*; only without the least trace of otherness can the Lord be seen, known and in essence entered. Such realization is possible only if the seeker has unswerving faith and earnestness of purpose. Without these twin virtues of faith and earnestness, no sustained effort is possible.

The *Gita* Parallels *A Course in Miracles*

The message of the Course is summarized in its introduction:

Nothing real can be threatened.
Nothing unreal exists.
Herein lies the peace of God.
T-In.2:2-3

Compare this to the message from the *Gita:* Of the non-existent there is no being, and of what exists there is no non-being; the definite ascertainment of both is seen by the seers of the essence of Truth (Ch. 2, verse 16).

The main practice in the Course is forgiveness, and its message is that one need do nothing except those activities which one's right mind (the Holy Spirit) directs. The message of the *Gita* is essentially the same: Perform your duties (action in the world) in a spirit of selfless service, abandoning all attachment to success or failure. Such equanimity is called yoga (union with God). This is action stemming from the right mind; this is similar to forgiveness in the Course.

> Update on the article, 2016: Since writing this article in 2004, the author has continued to be a student of both the Course and *Gita* and has arrived at a different understanding of the two, helped in large part by the teachings of Dr. David R. Hawkins, MD, PhD, whom the author saw for the first time in 2004. The author attended many lectures given by Dr. Hawkins during 2004 to 2011. In Dr. Hawkins the author found someone who was most intimately familiar with both the Course and *Gita*, demonstrating the teachings of both scriptures and elucidating the fine points of both while answering questions from live audiences. While both scriptures are written to take the student to a state of enlightenment, *Gita* is meant for more advanced students and discusses several items not touched upon in the Course, including more advanced states of Consciousness ("Infinite Supreme"), "Gunas" (attributes of Nature) and how to transcend them, how man can step up inner peace and usefulness to others and joy to himself, many tips and techniques for meditation and ways of reaching the divine goal, etc. Spiritual evolution takes place over long periods of time and the author is very grateful to have access to both the Course and *Gita*.

Arvind Kumar was born near New Delhi, India in 1951 and has been settled in the Dallas, Texas area since 1976, participating as a family man in various spiritual enrichment activities available through the Sufi, Hindu, Buddhist and Christian perspectives. In September 2004 Arvind attended a talk by Dr. David R. Hawkins, M.D., Ph.D, which changed the course of his life, as Dr. Hawkins presented an option to live life like a prayer, continuously forgiving, loving and giving, thereby becoming invulnerable to the perceptual world of senses, the stage on which the human dance continues to unfold seemingly endlessly. The author can be contacted via email at ak426@yahoo.com and welcomes follow-up questions or comments.

Chapter 3

Advaita Vedanta

David G. Brown

The Oneness of Non-Duality

The non-dual teachings of both Vedanta and *A Course in Miracles* present the awareness of Truth as Oneness, or the direct experience of God as undifferentiated Presence. This awareness of God, or Truth, as undifferentiated Oneness takes the place of the perception of God or Truth as being separate from who or what we think we are (apparently separated differentiated beings). Both forms of teaching (Vedanta and the Course) postulate that we are not physical bodies or even separated minds. However, we temporarily believe that we are individuals experiencing each other, as well as God, as objects in our awareness.

Both systems of teaching allow for a sense of gradually developing acceptance and perception of the world and each other, including God, as not separate from who we think we are. This misconception of separation is dependent only upon our unwillingness to let go of our "apparently" separate individualities. Ultimately, the teachings of both the Course and Vedanta tell us that the realization of Oneness supersedes all misconceptions of separation—thus resulting in a complete awareness of One Self, One God, One Presence, which is all there is.

Since most of us are not quite ready to let go of our individuality (and possibly fear the dissolution of what appears to be our separate self, or ego), both systems of teaching have a number of techniques and methods of unfolding these non-dual principles that help us transition from illusion to Truth. It is only in these methods, or techniques, that there is some divergence between the teachings of the Course and that of Vedanta. The ultimate aim of both these incredibly detailed and profound systems of metaphysical unfoldment is to replace our misunderstood acceptance of the world and ourselves as separated with a vision of Truth that is integrated, holistic and complete. In this awareness of Truth, all misguided appearances of sorrow and limitation (resulting from the thoughts of the separate ego-mind) end with a final wordless and thoughtless entry into the presence of Peace, Love and Joy.

So, having briefly described how these two systems' presentations of the goal of awakening are fundamentally the same, let us look at some of the differences between Vedanta and the Course, starting with a brief introduction of the origin and nature of Vedantic teaching.

Vedanta originated in India, probably more than five thousand years ago. It is part and parcel of a recorded system of ritualistic teachings and practices known as the Vedas. These ancient scriptures were originally transmitted orally and then written, becoming some of the earliest surviving records known to civilization. The language used in the Vedas is known as Sanskrit, which is still used today in many of the ashrams and academies all over the world where Vedanta is taught. I myself learned about Vedanta during the 1980's, when I was fortunate in being guided to a brilliant teacher, Swami Chinmayananda, with whom I traveled and studied for some years.

Fortunately for me, he taught Vedanta in English, liberally embellished with Sanskrit technical terms for which the English language does not provide an adequate reference. I have been a devoted student of Vedanta since that time, and still attend regular retreats with my present teacher, Swami Tejomayananda. Since I also was introduced to the Course and fell in love with its poetically lyrical rendition of Truth, I was blessed to find Ken Wapnick. My partner, Lynne, and I spent three years in Temecula, California, studying with him. So now I have to say that I am a student of both Vedanta and the Course.

Vedanta has been taught and practiced for many years and by many totally gifted and enlightened teachers for whom we are everlastingly grateful. Like the Course, Vedanta is a systematized method of imparting the wisdom of Truth without any of the embellishments of doctrine, practices or rituals. It was this purity that attracted me to Vedanta so many years ago, and it perhaps may be said that one of the hallmarks of a true teaching of Truth is the simplicity and directness of its principles and methods of attainment.

There are only a few core principles in Vedanta, one of which is the injunction to develop discrimination (*viveka*) and dispassion (*viragya*).

In the Course, as in Vedanta, discrimination means the ability to discern the ego thought system (deluded mind) and differentiate such thoughts from those of the right mind as guided by the Holy Spirit. In both Vedanta and the Course, discrimination and dispassion aid the student in choosing Truth over illusion. Both the Course and Vedanta encourage the willingness to put this realization of Truth into action by developing the capacity to move away from conditioning (identifying with the body) and attachments to the illusionary world of form. All of which, could be seen as learning to say "not no" to Truth, as Ken Wapnick often pointed out.

In both Vedanta and the Course, the student is constantly encouraged to keep a vision of Truth always at the front and center of thought and action. In Vedanta, the technical term for the Self is "*Atman*," which can be equated with the Course concept of the one "Son of God," an extension of God not separated from the universal Oneness. In the same way, Vedanta uses the term "*Iswara*" as the concept of a Creator and "*Brahman*" to refer to the non-differentiated principle of absolute Oneness, or God in the Course. Despite differences in terminology, the trinity in some form is therefore present in both the Course and Vedanta. However, the student quickly understands that these are terms put into place by the teaching to enable us to transition smoothly and comfortably (most of the time anyway) from the misunderstanding of separation to the direct awareness of unity.

Both systems often emphasize that the greatest obstacle to the practice of these teachings is our mindless acceptance of our own conditioning (that gives rise to the ego thought system), resulting in projection and judgment. So the "waking up" called for by Vedanta and the Course is firstly directed towards the increasing perception that nothing of this world is what it originally seems, and therefore is of the nature of an illusion. The Course applies the psychological principles so ably presented by Sigmund Freud, as well as the Biblical teachings of Jesus, utilized in ways that bring out their often hidden and deeper spiritual meaning.

In the same way, Vedanta draws on many psychological truths and insights in its various efforts to guide the student away from habituated thinking and unconscious patterns of behaviors. For example, in Vedantic teaching there are three main behavioral patterns representing either a lack of awareness or an ability for understanding: (1) an unconscious animal-based instinct of defense and attack (*tamas*); (2) an ego-based desire to judge and act selfishly (*rajas*); and (3) a receptive, open, and willing state of mind ready to listen to the teaching (*satwic*). The Course elaborates in ever deepening cycles of explanation and examples how these three major areas of personal awareness either guide us toward awakening (right-minded, *satwic*) or trap us into unhelpful behavior patterns (ego-based, *tamas* and *rajas*).

By using the Course text for study and the lessons for guiding our practice, the student is encouraged to make the subtle and sometimes gross changes that are needed for setting aside conditioned behavior and awakening to Truth. In Vedanta we see a similar approach spread over a number of texts, not just one book. The primary teaching of Vedanta is contained in twelve main volumes called Upanishads. There are many more books, but the content is clearly and completely presented in this smaller number. These texts were originally found in four main Vedic teachings which go back for four or five millennia.

Usually the Upanishads, the word meaning of which is "to sit near or beside a teacher," take the form of a dialogue between a student and teacher, in which students ask questions and demonstrate their willingness to learn and practice. In this way, the teaching unfolds from the relatively simple and straightforward explanations to the profoundest unfoldment of Truth possible, while still using words and symbols. These texts can still be used today to guide the modern teacher and student. With content similar to that of the Course, Vedantic teachings present an organized and logical unfoldment of the nature of the ego, the presence of misunderstanding and projection, and the final dawning of the realization that "what I am is the Truth Itself."

Contained in these sacred texts are the four primary principles of the teaching of Vedanta known as *Mahavakyas* or "great principles":

1. "Consciousness is Brahman." ("*Prajnanam Brahma.*") This means that there is nothing but the Oneness of the Absolute God known as Consciousness.
2. "That Thou Art." ("*Tat tvam asi.*") This means that even though you thought of yourself as a separated ego, in Truth you are none

other than this One Truth, everywhere present.

3. "This Self is Brahman." ("*Ayam Atma Brahma.*") This refers to the affirmation of awakening to the Truth.
4. "I am Brahman." ("*Aham Brahmasmi.*") This is the final direct awareness of the One Self everywhere present.

Compatible in content with "*My mind is part of God's. I am very holy*" (W-p.I.35.h), these teachings are only presented to the student when he or she is ready and open to receive them. We can see similar principles in the Course where the teacher, Jesus, refers to One-mindedness, or Heaven; wrong-mindedness, or the ego's thought system; and right-mindedness, which represents the thought system of the Holy Spirit (C-1.5-6). As previously mentioned, there is a correspondence between the terms of the Course (which are taken from Bible but re-purposed for a deeper metaphysical content) and those of Vedanta.

In both the Course and Vedanta, the reference to "knowledge" denotes a non-dual awareness of Truth and has nothing to do with the ego-mind that believes itself to be unique and separated. In practice, the use of words to communicate ideas can be both a blessing, because we need to communicate, and also a disadvantage, because of the limitation based upon interpretation by the listener and our own understanding.

Overcoming the limitation of words, Vedantic practice makes use of meditation as an additional aid to Truth realization. Vedanta advocates that the meditator focuses upon becoming the witness (*sakshi*), remaining the unattached perceiver of all appearances. This is an extension of the idea that the True Self is the witness of all objects and, therefore, can only be the unattached subject. Somewhat similarly, the Course advocates detaching, or standing back from, the turmoil of the ego-mind and resting in the peaceful center of our true Self. Additionally, early-on in the text, the Course gives the student this guideline: *"Be vigilant only for God and His Kingdom"* (T-6.V.C.h).

Vedanta calls for three main steps practiced in series as the effective means for realizing the Self as One's Self. They are (1) listening to a teacher or studying—*sravanam*; (2) reflection, contemplating upon what one has learned, including practicing—*mananam*; and

(3) meditation, including establishing one's self as the unattached witness—*nididhyasana*. The Workbook lessons of the Course, if practiced as instructed, include the essence of these three steps.

A discussion of Vedanta would be incomplete without a mention of the incomparable text attributed to the teacher Vyasa approximately 2,500 years ago, titled *The Bhagavad Gita*, which means "The Song of the Lord." This is a beautiful poetic text (in its Sanskrit format) in which a noble prince (Arjuna) is forced into a civil war where he has to choose between what he deems to be his just and proper duty as a warrior and the sorrow and conflict that war engenders. This scenario is generally seen as a simile for life in general in which these seemingly conflicting choices continually occur. In desperation, Arjuna turns to his charioteer, Krishna, who in a completely fortuitous way turns out to be an enlightened teacher in his own right.

Initially, Arjuna is ignorant of the nature of his illustrious companion and turns to him as a convenient listener; however, he quickly realizes that Krishna has an insight into the nature of all phenomena, as well as the ability to guide Arjuna in the realization of Truth. In the course of the eighteen chapters, we are witnesses to the unfoldment of Truth and the realization of the Self in the dialogue between Krishna and Arjuna. In this monumental teaching that has retained its glory and profound awareness for thousands of years, the figure of Krishna could be seen as a symbol for what the Course terms "the Holy Spirit," and Arjuna might be seen as a symbol for everyone in search of Self-realization.

The Course itself points out that there are many teachings on the realization of Truth, and once we find ourselves on the spiritual path, we will be guided to the teaching that will be most efficacious for us. The Introduction to the Course sums up the essence of its teaching (and that of all paths leading to Truth) as "*Nothing real can be threatened, nothing unreal exists. Herein lies the peace of God*" T-In.2:2-3). We need not use one teaching to justify the completeness of another, as the most important is the one that speaks to our hearts and minds. In other words, it becomes the vehicle for our own journey to take place.

I would like to close this comparison of the non-dual teachings of ACIM and Vedanta with a much-loved simile often presented in

Vedantic teaching sessions. True to the spirit of both Vedanta and the Course, this simile of the snake and the rope captures and resolves the seeming conflict between Reality and illusion:

The Snake and the Rope

The misunderstanding, or misperception, of the world is technically referred to in Vedanta as a "superimposition," because all illusions require some underlying support in order for them to appear to exist. Various examples of this superimposition are the mirage in the desert, which requires the heated floor of the desert to distort and reflect a far distant oasis. A rainbow requires the presence of sunlight and water vapor. A horror movie requires our participation in converting the images on the screen into a fearful story that we happily leave behind at the theatre when the film has ended. In other words, the illusion of a mirage is superimposed on the heated desert floor, as the illusion of a rainbow is superimposed on sunlight and water vapor. The movie screen itself is an example of superimposition—it is needed to see images that do not exist in physical form on the screen.

Some common questions raised by students of Vedanta and the Course are, "Why or how did this world of separation happen?" or "Why did God create this world?" Of course, we can see that these questions are being asked by the ego's thought system, which is already making something up and taking the misperception seriously. So, often the teacher, realizing the nature of the question, uses the following example of superimposition to illustrate a response:

Imagine that I walk into a darkened room or perhaps my garage at night. In the corner of the room, I see a coiled object on the floor, and the first thought that comes to mind is that it's a snake—perhaps poisonous or ready to attack and bite. What do I do? Should I run, or find a stick or something to hit it with, or even perhaps try to kill it? My heart is beating quickly, my muscles are tense with the fight or flight responses. I cannot find a stick or any object in the gloomy room. I must first turn on a light, while carefully watching to see that the snake does not suddenly attack or, more likely, find a spot to hide where I cannot get to it without some risk to myself. Slowly, carefully, I find the light switch next to the door I came in and flick it on!

I look for the snake and what do I see—a small coil of rope in the corner! I laugh out loud with relief, while at the same time releasing the tension in my body and feeling some sense of having been taken in by my fearful illusion.

What happened to the snake? Now I see that it never existed; there was no snake. It is not as though there really were a snake that crawled away and hid somewhere. No! It never was there in the first place. The only thing that existed was the rope, which never changed. However, without the rope I could not have superimposed, or imagined, a fearsome snake upon the rope's coils.

This example of a rope appearing to be a non-existent snake demonstrates the nature of all illusion. The illusion of the rope being a snake (like all fearful illusions) had a temporary seeming reality which was disturbing or fearsome because of my belief in its reality. But when the true nature of the image (the rope) was brought to light and made clear, the misperception of the snake completely disappeared. The snake (or illusion) was not destroyed, replaced, superseded or forgotten; it was seen to be what it is—nothing!

Ultimately, the concept of superimposition explains that we actually perceive the Truth, or Reality, in all appearances. However, because of our own mental confusion, we imagine a series of impressions or projections to make appear what can never be more than an illusion. We superimpose our thoughts and state of mind onto the world and then misperceive it for Reality.

> *Projection makes perception. The world you see is what you gave it, nothing more than that. But though it is no more than that, it is not less. Therefore, to you it is important. It is the witness to your state of mind, the outside picture of an inward condition.*
>
> **T-21.In.1:1-5**

David G. Brown currently lives in south Florida with his loving companion Lynne. David has been a student of Vedanta since the early 1980's. Following a "Miracles" seminar by Jon Mundy in 2006, David and Lynne spent three years in Temecula, CA studying *A Course in Miracles* with Ken Wapnick. Current activities include facilitating study groups in both Vedanta and *A Course in Miracles*, editing Course books, and writing.

Chapter 4

Yoga

Rev. Amy Torres

A Course in Miracles offers us a highly individualized curriculum where we use the body as a learning device under the direction of the Holy Spirit. Yoga is one of the classrooms the Holy Spirit offers me to use my body for spiritual purposes. The Course provides mind-training; therefore, all of its practices are in thought-form, or ideas. This can be challenging, since the body demands our attention all day long. Yoga offers a body-based *sadhana*, or spiritual practice, using the body and breath to reconnect with God's Mind. This way, instead of letting the body run the show, we have concrete techniques so the body serves the Mind.

> *The body, valueless and hardly worth the least defense, need merely be perceived as quite apart from you, and it becomes a healthy, serviceable instrument through which the mind can operate until its usefulness is over.*
>
> **W-p.I.135.8:2**

Most of us think of yoga as a physical practice, but the physical movements or *asanas*, known as *hatha yoga*, are but one of five yoga systems. Hindu philosophy speaks of *hatha yoga, raja yoga, bhakti yoga, jnana yoga, and karma yoga.* Each of these systems can be used autonomously to realize God, or they can be used in combination. Yoga comes from the Sanskrit word "yuj" which means "to yoke" or "join" as in union with our brothers and communion with God.

Swami Satchidananda defines yoga as "the science of mind" and explains that "the mind is a veil woven with thoughts." Yoga is a system that helps us harness the mind, because as long as the ego mind gives us the runaround, we remain unaware of the One Mind in which we all truly live. As Jesus says, in a section of his Course called, "The Lifting of the Veil":

Together we will disappear into the Presence beyond the veil, not to be lost but found; not to be seen but known.

T-19.IV.D.i.19:1

In addition to the five well-known yogic systems mentioned above, there is *kundalini yoga, tantric yoga, kriya yoga*, and the list goes on. Yoga is a vast subject and there are countless books and online resources to explore *karma*, the *chakras*, kundalini energy and the *koshas*, as well as many other esoteric topics, if you are so inclined. David Hoffmeister has an interesting chart in his book, *Awakening Through A Course in Miracles*, that maps the ego mind, and the layers are remarkably similar to the koshas. The koshas are the five layers of mental and physical being which comprise the personal self, the Atman (Christ Self) being at the center.

Hatha Yoga

Hatha yoga is the *physical movement* of yoga, the asanas, or postures. It is said that *rishis*, the Hindu mystics of five thousand years ago, inadvertently "invented" hatha yoga when they surfaced from deep meditation and felt stiff. The stretching they did to limber up was based on what they saw around them in nature: they mimicked animals, mountains, and trees to loosen up and invigorate the body. Nowadays, hatha yoga is used as preparation for meditation. It can also be seen as a moving meditation in itself. When the movements are linked to the breath, and smooth transitions melt one pose into the next, the mind is smoothed also. Relaxing and strengthening the body can be a way of calming the mind, which helps us harness our thoughts and concentrate, the entry to meditation. In the Course, Jesus agrees that we are much too tolerant of mind wandering. On the other hand, although there is a structured exercise practice in the Workbook lessons, Jesus is not strict about a formal ongoing meditation practice.

Nor is a lifetime of contemplation and long periods of meditation aimed at detachment from the body necessary. All such attempts will ultimately succeed because of their purpose. Yet the means are tedious and very time consuming, for all of them look to the future for release from a state of present unworthiness and inadequacy.

T-18.VII.4:9-11

Yoga is an unhurried, ancient practice based, to some extent, on an accumulation of good karma. It takes time to balance chakras, activate kundalini energy, and transcend the sheaths of the *koshas*. The Course is a refreshing counterbalance to yoga in that it promises to save us time.

> *You are not making use of the course if you insist on using means which have served others well, neglecting what was made for you. Save time for me by only this one preparation, and practice doing nothing else. "I need do nothing" is a statement of allegiance, a truly undivided loyalty. Believe it for just one instant, and you will accomplish more than is given to a century of contemplation, or of struggle against temptation. To do nothing is to rest, and make a place within you where the activity of the body ceases to demand attention. Into this place the Holy Spirit comes, and there abides.*
>
> T-18.VII.6:5-8; 7:7-8.

Interestingly, the final resting pose in hatha yoga is the most important; the entire asana practice culminates in *savasana*, corpse pose, in which the fruits of practice are absorbed. Similarly, after completing the Workbook and learning that we "rest in God" and "need do nothing" we let the Holy Spirit use the body as a vehicle through which God's Unifying Love flows.

Bhakti Yoga

Bhakti yoga is a path of selfless devotion to God. Krishna's *gopis* exemplified bhakti yoga. Gopi means "cowherding girl." Folklore holds that when Krishna played his flute, gopi women dropped what they were doing, whether it was cooking, tending to the cows, or washing clothes. Everything would be left in the middle and the gopis would abandon their families to dance ecstatically around Krishna as he seduced them with his flute. At night, Krishna would visit every gopi and make love to her.

Historically, Mirabai, the thirteenth-century mystic poet, valued her symbolic spiritual marriage to Krishna over her family's arranged marriage for her. She spurned convention, surrendered entirely to her passion for Lord Krishna, and experienced Love alternately through knowing It, and yearning for It. The Course asks us for the same level of devotion. Lesson 157, "*Into His Presence would I enter now,*" expresses it this way:

> *From this day forth, your ministry takes on a genuine devotion, and a glow that travels from your fingertips to those you touch, and blesses those you look upon.*
>
> W-P.I.157.5:1

Bhakti yoga has a quality of unreserved love and passion for God, a full faith that recognizes that God comes first.

Jnana Yoga

Jnana yoga uses the study of scripture as a means to comprehend our true Self. What starts out as an intellectual pursuit deepens into a felt experience. Jnana uses inquiry to uncover meaning *beneath* meaning and *beyond* meaning until the Self is revealed. The great sage and realized master Ramana Maharshi taught through the question, "Who am I?" This question, aimed at everything, takes us back to Witnessing, Observing, Awareness. In the Course, Jesus calls it "the power of decision" to align your mind with God-Mind by choosing Love rather than fear. This choice undoes the veils that the ego has interposed between its little slice of mind and its Source. Jnana yoga undoes the belief in personal identity by stripping away the false self, layer by layer.

> *This single purpose [stripping away the false self] creates perfect integration and establishes the peace of God.*
>
> T-3.II.5:6

Ultimately, Jesus advises,

> *Forget this world, forget this course, and come with wholly empty hands unto your God.*
>
> W-P.I.189.7:5

Until we reach total surrender, immersing ourselves in scripture can be the royal road Home. This may begin as an intellectual pursuit, but when done sincerely, intellect is used in service of Wisdom. Rather than be lost in the ego's "brainy" unconscious, we can choose to saturate ourselves in the Holy Spirit's all-inclusive Intelligence and higher consciousness.

Karma Yoga

Karma yoga is the yoga of taking action in the world through selfless service. It is a pure practice of brotherhood. It is the natural expression of the miracle, seeing Christ in everyone, indiscriminately. It is the application of generalization.

> *You will recognize that you have learned there is no order of difficulty in miracles when you apply them to all situations. There is no situation to which miracles do not apply, and by applying them to all situations, you will gain the real world.*
>
> T-12.VII.1:3-4

Jesus calls karma yoga "forgiveness" in the Course, and advises us to see the Christ in each other and discover we, just like he, are Christ.

Raja Yoga

Patanjali, the sage who compiled the Yoga Sutras, lays out the path of *raja yoga*. Raja means *royal* and is considered *a complete system*. Its goal is to improve our concentration so we can move all our attention toward our Being in order to realize we *are* that Being. Raja yoga is also called *ashtanga yoga* because of the eight limbs on which the system rests: They are:

1. *Yamas*—outward morality, consisting of non-harming, truthfulness, non-stealing, self-discipline and non-coveting;
2. *Niyamas*—inner ethics, consisting of cleanliness, contentment, purification of body, mind and nervous system, study of metaphysical principles and self-examination, contemplation of God;
3. *Asanas*—physical movements and postures;
4. *Pranayama*—control of breath and life currents;
5. *Pratyahara*—withdrawal of the senses in order to turn within;

6. *Dharana*—concentration, which lays the groundwork for meditation;
7. *Dhyana*—prolonged periods of concentration, also called meditation;
8. *Samadhi*—what the Course calls "revelation," a direct experience of God.

As Jesus says in the *Clarification of Terms, "A universal theology is impossible, but a universal experience is not only possible but necessary"* (C-In.2:5). Similar to raja yoga, ACIM also has a curriculum, and uses a text, workbook, and manual for teachers as its "limbs," which, when used vigilantly, integrate its teachings and deepen our learning (which is actually an unlearning). The Course curriculum is devoted to removing the blocks to the awareness of Love's presence, and, in so doing, reveals the Love (itzvot) that is our true natural state.

The Yoga of ACIM

Though I was introduced to yoga first, along the way it became clear to me that ACIM is my path. The lack of ceremony and ritual, the lack of deities and complicated practices, suits me. I have a gypsy nature, which finds the "no baggage" style of Jesus' Course a natural fit.

Somehow the Holy Spirit synthesized yoga and ACIM within me, and now it comes naturally to practice "ACIM yoga." In fact, this is how I was led to follow the great contemporary mystic, Sri Mooji (see video, "Thunderbolts of Truth and Blessings to ACIM Students" on YouTube).

Be it immersion in ACIM scripture, moving meditation, forgiveness opportunities, or mantra chanting (see video, "Prescription for Inner Peace" on YouTube), I find that aligning with Spirit has to help us relinquish identifying as "somebody" and discover "no body."

ACIM bhakti yoga emerged effortlessly too, as it became natural to devote the fruits of my practice to God. ACIM jnana yoga is the pleasure of reading and re-reading the Course, experiencing a deeper and deeper understanding, as well as cultivating the relationship with my guru, the Universal Guide, the Holy Spirit, who may be encountered in disembodied masters, such as Jesus, or embodied masters, such as Mooji.

ACIM raja yoga is applying the practices, the Workbook lessons, and allowing the Course to work through me as an integrated whole. ACIM karma yoga is seeing Christ in my brother. And ACIM hatha yoga literally reversed my upside-down perception when I used to do headstands. Plus, every practice concludes with evoking the Holy Instant by chanting "*AUM*."

Not so long ago, I observed myself giving a guided meditation to my yoga class during the final resting pose, savasana. A Quiet Confidence, warm yet impersonal, put words in my mouth, inviting the students to contact a glowing light within them that is always there. Conscious contact with this inner light allowed it to permeate and heal their bodies. Next, it extended radiantly through them and beyond them, making their very presence a source of healing to all they came in contact with the rest of the day (and perhaps much longer than a day).

"The light is in you," I said, channeling a line from Chapter 18. "You need do nothing except not to interfere," I continued, transmitting Chapter 16 from the "True Empathy" section. The Light flowed through me on Its way to them, for we are always within that Light. How liberating "to let my words be chosen for me by ceasing to decide for myself what I'm going to say" (paraphrased from M-21).

In conclusion, please accept my "*Namaste*," the Sanskrit word for, "The divine Light in me bows to the divine Light in you," or, in ACIM-speak,

> *You are one Self with me, united with our Creator in this self. I honor you because of What I am, and What He is, Who loves us both as One.*
>
> **W-P.I.95.15:3**

Rev. Amy Torres is a spiritual teacher, interfaith minister and retired *Gestalt* psychotherapist and yoga instructor. She writes the popular *Ask Amy* column in *Miracles* magazine. Her book, *Sweet Dreams of Awakening: 365 Good Night Blessings*, is a perfect companion to the ACIM Workbook, and her e-course, *Workin' the Workbook*, offers over 365 videos to support your workbook practice. Subscribe to her free e-newsletter, *The Unlearning Classroom*, at www.amytorresacim.com.

Chapter 5

Buddhism

Rev. Laura Derr, Ph.D.

The basic philosophical foundation between Budddhism and *A Course in Miracles* is the same, and there is enormous consistency between their teachings and practices, though there are some significant differences. I grew up with parents who met in a Protestant Christian seminary, so church was a big focus of our family life. As an adult I practiced mindfulness meditation with a Buddhist sangha in the tradition of Thich Nhat Hanh for 20 years. About 10 years ago I found the Course and experienced it as a connecting link between my Christian roots and my adult Buddhist practice. From the vantage point of being familiar with both Buddhism and Western Christianity, I have found that the Course is far more akin to the former than the latter, and I found that my studies of Buddhism made it easy for me to absorb Jesus' teachings in the Course.

Buddhism in a Nutshell

"Everything arises in the mind," so taught the World-Honored Lord Gautama, the Enlightened One, the Buddha, who lived in northern India about 2600 years ago.

The Buddha taught that the mind in which everything arises is one unified mind, and it projects the illusion of time and space, that is, everything our senses show us in our universe, including matter and our experience of each person having a separate consciousness. This projection process is driven by the delusion that everything has a separate self. As soon as there is the thought of separation, the fear of the loss of that separate self arises, producing all manner of negative thoughts and feelings, including desire, greed, fear, hatred, and anger. These states of mind create the conditions for the next state of mind to arise, deeply reinforcing our belief in the reality of our delusions. Moreover, we are ignorant of this projection process and what drives it (called *dependent co-arising*), and without spiritual guidance, we will continue to repeat the cycle of birth and death through this world of suffering, called *samsara*. This is the teaching of *karma*—that all events are consequences of our thoughts and actions, which are connected in web-like fashion throughout space and time, all of which is simultaneous in infinite directions and dimensions. All events are, thus, opportunities to experience and undo the knots and obstacles that exist in our belief system, and to be grateful for the process.

Gautama Buddha emphasized that the world is an illusion, as evanescent as a drop of dew or a flash of lightning In fact, the *Three Dharma Seals*—ideas by which one can know that a teaching is the truth—are *non-self* (nothing is separate in space), *impermanence* (nothing is separate in time), and *Nirvana* (the truth behind the illusion, the oneness of everything).

Behind this veil of illusion—*the historical dimension*—is Nirvana, which means the absence of all ideas, the absence of all concepts, direct knowledge, perfect understanding. This is the ultimate dimension which is our true home. It is not describable in words, but attempts are made, such as *primordial unconditioned awareness, Wisdom Mind, Buddha Mind,* or the *nature of awakening*. Enlightenment is the experience of being in touch with Nirvana directly. It is described that, with diligent practice, moments of touching Nirvana can increase in frequency until one is able to attain the state of living there continuously. Paradoxically, one realizes that there was nothing to attain, that Nirvana has existed in us all along.

In Buddhist psychology, consciousness has four levels, *Store Consciousness, Mind Consciousness, Manas, and Sense Consciousnesses.*

Store Consciousness is the root of all levels of consciousness, the continuous background that never ceases flowing, no matter what the condition of the other levels. In Western psychology, the term *unconscious* has some similarities, though Store has a much more vital function in Buddhist psychology. All information brought in through Mind and Sense Consciousnesses are processed by Store with no filtering. In a sense, it is victim to whatever we put into it. It organizes and maintains all inputs acquired from our experiences and from the collective Store of other people—there is no line between the individual and collective Store. Store is the level on which karma is operating, the infinitely complex interactions between individual and collective.

Manas is the mediator between Store Consciousness and Mind Consciousness. Known as *the Lover*, Manas looks at Store, the collective mind, and grasps a piece of it—the thought *I am*—and views it as its *self*, claiming it as its own. It becomes enamored of its illusory object of attachment, becomes fearful of losing it, and so works diligently to maintain its survival. All sorts of damaging states of mind arise from this effort, including things we think of as normal, such as self-esteem, the ideas of *me* and *mine*, and judgments about the relative goodness or value of things. Manas does not know that it is entirely deluded in its perception of having a separate self, that its object of attachment is only an image it has created, not a correct perception of reality.

Mind Consciousness is the level that is operating when we are awake or dreaming, but not in deep sleep or a coma. This is the level in which we have a choice about where to place our attention, about whether to be mindful or driven by unwholesome mental states. Because Mind directs the actions of body, speech, and thought, which, thus, reinforce the condition of Store, it is critical to practice mindfulness. Mind is called *the Gardener* because it cultivates Store. Store will manifest what we choose, regardless of whether or not we are aware of what we are choosing.

The level of *Sense Consciousness* comes from contact of a sense organ with an object it can recognize. When eyes see a form, eye consciousness arises; when ears hear a sound, ear consciousness is the result, and so on. The objects of perception *do not exist separately* from the Sense Consciousness that perceives them.

Parallels between Buddhism and *A Course in Miracles*

Readers who are familiar with the Course will have already noticed the multiple congruencies between these two thought-systems. Both are founded in the understanding of the oneness of time, space and mind. They agree on the cause of the creation of the universe—an illusion arising from the deluded, mad idea of separateness. Buddhism, which has had 2,600 years to evolve in the context of many cultures, may describe this process in more detail, but it agrees with the Course that understanding the workings of this projection process is important only insofar as this helps us not be attached to the world. What is most important is to cultivate the correct state of mind that will allow us to get out of this mess. Both are active learning programs, both describing the spiritual path as a practice of mind-training. Both emphasize the necessity of letting go of attachment to worldly things, focusing instead on the state of our minds.

Some of the methods of mind-training are similar, and some differ. Over the centuries, Buddhism has developed many techniques for maintaining our awareness in the present moment, beginning with the Buddha's teaching of the full awareness of breathing. In this teaching, he directs us not only to pay attention to our body, our feelings, our mind, and our thoughts, but to actively cultivate thoughts about the impermanence of everything, the disappearance of desire, and the letting go of all attachments to what we believe is our own separate body and mind.

In the Course, Jesus does not use the technique of awareness of breath and body, emphasizing instead that the body is not real, it is purely a manifestation of ego, and that the best use of our awareness is to focus on listening to and trusting Holy Spirit. Like the Buddha, he supplies us with concepts that are aids in undoing our confusions and delusions, guideposts on the path of cultivating our ability to experience Truth. Both masters emphasize the necessity of listening to our inner wisdom, and not listening to ego or *manas*. Both describe ego/manas as vicious and dangerous, as greedy, always wanting more, and never satisfied, like a fire that burns ceaselessly. Both describe the great difficulty in escaping its clever grasp.

Some terms that are important to both systems are used to convey the same concepts. *Enlightenment* in Buddhism is *salvation* in the Course, the experience of being identified with the One Wisdom Mind, no longer having any attachment to the idea of separateness. This Wisdom Mind, or Buddha Nature, that Buddhism describes as permeating everything, is the *Holy Spirit* in the Course. Those moments when Mind Consciousness is in touch with Store Consciousness would be what the Course describes as the *Holy Instant.*

Jesus describes the Holy Spirit in more *active* terms than Buddhism describes the Wisdom Mind. Both indicate that It is always loving and always available to the quiet mind willing to listen, but Jesus emphasizes Spirit's miraculous helpfulness: Its delight in using our little bit of willingness to provide us with deeply healing experiences; Its happiness to provide us with guidance whenever we ask; Its joy in our deepening trust. The Buddha knew well that people who had attained a certain level of spiritual awareness could perform miracles, but he admonished his students not to do this because he considered it a distraction from attaining deeper levels of awareness; also, it made others believe it was magic, and not a manifestation of the mind to which everyone has access.

There is a significant difference between these spiritual systems regarding God. The Course describes the Holy Spirit as the link between our apparently separated minds and the Mind of God. The Buddha carefully avoided the word *God* in describing the Wisdom Mind, for reasons that a scholar of Buddhism might know, but I do not. My strong hunch is that he wanted to emphasize that Nirvana, our true home, is already within our minds, and if he used *God*, people might think of God as separate from and external to themselves, and thus distract themselves from the true purpose of his teaching, which was to provide us with a path out of suffering. I think that Nirvana might be thought of as the Son of God, the mind that has all the power of love and creation, (including the power to delude itself that it does not), but that did not create itself.

The Buddha and Jesus both describe this mind masterfully, and both carefully avoid trying to describe God. The Buddha wisely said nothing, and Jesus often said that the moment of returning to the knowledge of God cannot be described. All we can say is, "*God is*" (W-p.I.169.5:4). Jesus' description of God needing us to return home in order for God to be complete, of God weeping at the "sacrifice" of His children who believe they are lost to Him, are not ideas that the Buddha taught. Though the Buddha did not say that Nirvana needs us to return home, he did emphasize that the true homecoming will only occur when all sentient beings have been enlightened.

Here is where these two spiritual systems differ significantly. Jesus needed the concepts of God and His realm to describe ego dynamics. The Course states we believe that we have attacked God and usurped

His power, which has resulted in our profound feelings of guilt and our fear of retaliation, a fear that is so acute, it is projected outwards. All the complex machinations of the ego to ward off this imagined retaliation is unique to the Course. For example, the Buddha would certainly describe bodily illness as a manifestation of Store Consciousness in concert with Manas and Mind; whereas, Jesus describes it as a manipulation of the ego to mitigate its imagined punishment by God by punishing itself first. In so doing, the ego arrogantly believes it has the power to appease God and control God's actions. While the Buddha did not use the same terminology of attack and its utter lack of justification, he thoroughly described the power of negative emotions and states-of-mind to maintain suffering, and he constantly emphasized the necessity of cultivating the mind of love. Jesus tells us we are sinless because this whole illusory universe never happened in reality. The concept of sin does not exist in Buddhism, though its description of our habitual creation of suffering would be a close equivalent.

Both of these great teachings emphasize the reality of love and its cultivation as the path out of our belief in sin and suffering. We are here due to the erroneous perception of separation, and our spiritual purpose is to remove the blocks to our understanding of the unifying Truth of love. The difference between these two great teachings is only a matter of technique or emphasis. The Course repeatedly stresses that we must practice forgiving ourselves and others, based in the understanding that there is no distinction between self and other, that we are creating our experience of separateness through our repetitive thoughts about attack and defense.

The stakes are high: as we forgive, we undo these separation thoughts and allow Truth to become visible; as long as we don't forgive, we remain in hell. One manifestation of hell is the belief in specialness, which only reinforces our differences and, thus, our separation. Ceasing to use relationships to reinforce the specialness the ego craves is of critical necessity on the path towards salvation. Buddhism has a lovely practice called *metta* that consists of sending thoughts of love, well-being, protection and happiness to others, including those whom we perceive as being the cause of our suffering. Though a bit less active in its implementation, it is very similar to the Course's practice of forgiveness, and is based in the identical understanding that the other is myself.

The difference in these practices is one of degree, but it has resulted in some huge differences in the forms of spiritual practice. Jesus teaches us to engage with others regularly, for it is in these engagements that the opportunities to practice forgiveness will arise. While the Buddha strongly emphasized sangha practice and he himself organized a community of many hundreds of monastics whom he instructed to help each other in their practice of the Dharma. Over the centuries, the practice of meditation has become more solitary, more of an encounter with our own minds, and a disengagement from the world. Because Buddhism has such a long history and many variations, there is disagreement on whether to emphasize individual or collective practice.

Jesus tells us that the ego loves complexity. I could spend a lifetime elucidating the permutations of parallels and variations between the teachings of Gautama Buddha and Jesus. I see, however, that they are teaching us the same thing: there is only the perfect oneness of loving wisdom.

Rev. Laura Derr, Ph.D. is a clinical psychologist in the Boston area. She began her study and practice of Buddhism while in graduate school, so the perspective of this philosophy has been intimately intertwined with her understanding of psychological practice. More recently, she has found a further body of Jesus' modern teachings in the *Way of Mastery,* which she feels is even more closely aligned with Buddhism than *A Course in Miracles.* In *The Way of Mastery,* Jesus teaches the Buddhist practice of mindfulness of the breath and body, first as the means to finding the mental obstacles that need healing, and then as the means to experiencing the love, light and breath of God directly. Laura is currently a student at the All Faiths International Seminary. doctor.derr@gmail.com

Chapter 6

After Enlightenment, Zen What?

Jon Mundy, Ph.D.

A Very Short History of Zen Buddhism

Buddha lived and taught in India during the 5th century B.C.E. In the 2nd century C.E., Buddhism moved from India over the Himalayan mountains into Tibet and China. There, part of the Mahayana branch of Buddhism mixed with the Chinese philosophy of Taoism and came to be known as *Chan*. The Chan movement then crossed into Japan in the 12th century where it was again influenced this time by the ancient Shinto religion's deep appreciation for natural order and Chan became known as Zen. Zen places an emphasis on quietude of mind and rigorous meditation as the most direct method for stopping the mind's insane machinations, thus, bringing us to peace.

Tommyrot

An English Minister of the Gospel was conducting religious services at a senior citizen residence when suddenly his discourse was interrupted by one of the residents crying out, "I say! Have we got to listen to this tommyrot?" The minister, surprised and confused, looked to the resident supervisor and said, "Shall I stop speaking?" The supervisor replied, "Keep right on. That won't happen again. That man has only one sane moment every couple of years."

The first time I saw those two airplanes flying into the World Trade Center, two lines from the Course passed through my mind:

> *Do not underestimate the intensity of the ego's drive for vengeance on the past.*
> **T-16.VII.3:1**

and

> *This is an insane world, and do not underestimate the extent of its insanity.*
> **T-14.I.2:6**

Of all of the major religions of the world, Buddhism has been the most peaceful. Both Zen and the Course, recognizing the insanity of this world and call upon our use of reason to help us come to a peaceful mind. What is called for is "undoing" or "unlearning" as according to both Zen and the Course,

The memory of God comes to the quiet mind.

T-23.I.1:1

"Sitting quietly, doing nothing, Spring comes,
and the grass grows by itself."

The Zenrin-kushu, an Anthology of Zen Passages

Zen, like the Course, seeks to bring sanity to the world by dropping judgment. "Look without any ideas," says Zen. Look on the world without prejudice. Let there be no presuppositions—no good, no bad. When we have judgment, we have problems—we have separation, we have division, we have duality. Just look—sit still—let things be what they are.

"The whole of life is diseased. If I were a doctor
and I were asked my advices I would say, 'Create Silence.'"

~Danish Theologian, Soren Kierkegaard (1813-1855)

A quiet mind is a reasonable mind. A quiet mind is a sane mind. It is not until we can still the mind, not until we can stop incessant ego-chatter that we have a real opportunity to see. There is a saying in Zen, "Your own mind—this is Buddha." From the standpoint of the Course we might say, "Your own mind—this is Christ."

This idea of passing may be called time,
but it is an incorrect idea,
for since one sees it only as passing,
one cannot understand that it stays just where it is.

~Zen Master, Dogen (1200-1253)

No Time but Now

Like the Course, Zen speaks of the insubstantiality of the individual ego and the ephemeral nature of time. Hinduism, Buddhism, and the Course all speak of this world as a phenomenal world, a dream world, maya or illusion. Don Miguel Ruiz, in his book, *The Four Agreements,* talks about what he calls *domestication* or *the dreaming of the planet.* We are currently living in what might be called the Western 21st Century System of Glossing, that is, we are experiencing the world as it is being made up at the beginning of the 21st century, a world very different from, say, the way it was being made up 100 years ago when the world was caught in the middle of World War I (1914-1918). This is an insane world simply because it is the ego's world. It always has been.

Each generation is taught the ways of the world over and over again until we overlearn the way of world, i.e. the ego. As the song from *South Pacific* said it, "You have to be carefully taught; you have to be taught to hate and fear; you have to be carefully taught." Everyone is born a mystic; then we take the child off to the school—we study history, we learn right and wrong and the conclusion is—you, whoever you are, you who are different from me. You are wrong.

Make Believe

In 1958, Country Music Singer, Conway Twitty (1933-1993), had a number one hit song titled, *Make Believe*, in which he bemoaned the fact that all the hopes and dreams he had about a possible loving relationship were—only make-believe. "*My only prayer will be, . . . someday you'll care for me, but it's o o o only . . . make-believe.*" Zen says, "Be in the world but don't be *of* the world." Don't be caught in make-believe. There is no need to renounce the world—just see its illusory nature and let it be. That which needs to be fixed isn't in the world—it's in the mind. Thus, Mahatma Gandhi can say, *"Be the change you want to see."*

The Kingdom of Heaven is inside where God is. Heaven is in the Mind. It is not a place. It is an awareness of Perfect Oneness. It's simply a matter of choice. What do I wish to see? Where shall I look for direction in my seeing? The outside world is a place of politics, competition and battles where egos play games of intrigue and strategy, all for the purpose of obtaining wealth, power and control.

> *Many have chosen to renounce the world while still believing its reality. And they have suffered from a sense of loss, and*

have not been released accordingly. Others have chosen nothing but the world, and they have suffered from a sense of loss still deeper, which they did not understand. Between these paths there is another road that leads away from loss of every kind, for sacrifice and deprivation both are quickly left behind. This is the way appointed for you now.
W-P.I.155.4:2-4; 5:1-2

Buddha's great enlightenment was that all of life is desiring, attachment and suffering. The ego's attachments to idols, things, status, power, and our many complicated relationships keep us distracted and we don't even see sanity.

Words Start the World

Projection makes perception. The world is as we make it, as we see it, project or intend it. The ego has a host of projective, "name calling" words in its arsenal. Words like sleazy, pathetic, stupid, insane, ludicrous, ridiculous, idiotic, and absurd. All such projections simply keep us from blinded by our own prejudice.

According to the Course, the most basic law there is in the universe is the law of cause and effect. As we give, so do we receive. As we pardon, so are we pardoned. By loving what is in front of me, love will come my way. The ego flips this law around backward and rather than making life a win-win it becomes a lose-lose. Attack and be attacked. If I must lose then so will you. This is the way of war. No one wins at war. War is justified murder. War is hell and everyone loses.

Devise No Words

After my near-death experience in 1976, I could not talk because I realized that anything I said would be a construct, that is, an attempt to try to put into words the description of an experience which did not fit into words. Bodhidharma, the legendary founder of Zen, said, "Devise no words." This state is called "mo chao"—when we are not projecting. "Mo" means serene or silent and "chao" means awareness. It means a mirror-like quality—just reflect. Just observe says Zen without comment or commentary—without appraisal, assessment or analysis.

Words are symbols of symbols—twice removed from reality (M-21.1:9-10). Words start the world. The moment we enter the world of words, the world begins and soon there are many words, argumentation and alienation. My wife Dolores' favorite line from the Course is:

> *Let him (her) be what he (she) is, and seek not to make of love an enemy*
>
> T-19.IV.Di.13:8

Reality is Intrinsic

God cannot be theologized, speculated on, or argued about. Thus, Jesus tells us, "I Kingdom of Heaven is inside you." It's not in our bodies. It's not in the world. It's in The Mind—which is now and has forever been the One and only Reality. Truth is not out there. Truth is in this moment—in my immediate experience; in my mind. The more awake I am, the more aware I am, the deeper the appreciation and gratitude for what has been given.

It's Not About Theology

A Christian theologian was attending a conference on world religions in Tokyo. He went up to a Shinto master and said, "I 'on't think I get your ideology. I 'on't understand your theology." The Shinto master looked at him for a moment and said, "I don't think we have a theology. I don't think we have an ideology. We dance."

> *A universal theology is impossible, but a universal experience is not only possible but necessary.*
>
> C-In.2:5

Zen is Not a Theology

Zen is simple, pure, absolute, and inculpable religion. Words easily become pollutants. Theologizing contaminates and spoils religion. Theology is something about which we might have debates. People have been arguing for centuries because of "dogmas," ideologies, geocentricism, ego-centrism, nationalism, communism—"any-ism" will do. Zen is more like love. Try to define it. You'll lose it. We can't be in Spirit and in ego at the same time. A house divided against itself cannot stand.

> *There is no answer; only an experience. Seek only this, and do not let theology delay you.*
>
> **C-IN.4:4-5**

Mysticism Has No Theology

Mysticism is a direct experience. Mystics have truth. They have luminosity. They do not have doctrine. They do not have dogma. There is no creed, no canon, no set code of beliefs. There is no required way of believing. There is simply seeing, which transcends agreement and disagreement. The Course says, *The ego analyzes; the Holy Spirit accepts* (T-11.V.13:1). Zen says 'on't dissect, 'on't analyze. To analyze is to separate, to break down, to tear apart but God cannot be divided. God is the whole, not the part. God can be found only in a vision of Unity.

Zen is an experience. The Course is an experience. The more you practice Zen and the more you study the Course, the deeper the experience. The more peaceful you become. There is no church in Zen and no Pope. In the same way, the Course is a self-study. There is no pecking order, no chain-of-command. The moment we create a hierarchy, egos get involved.

> *I have nothing that does not come from God. The difference between us now is that I have nothing else. This leaves me in a state which is only potential in you.*
>
> **T-1.II:3.11-13**

All that is needed is to step back and let truth come naturally into view. Zen has not become a tradition like Christianity and Judaism. It cannot. The Course will not become a tradition either. It is simply a study and a way of seeing in which glimpses of Heaven begin coming into view.

Like Zen, the Course is subtle. It all happens inside. The more you hang in there, the quieter the mind becomes even in the midst of busyness. The Course, like Zen, is a way of Being. No one is special. We are all equal brothers and sisters. What Jesus has seen, we might see. What Jesus has done, we might do. Looking out on the world with loving eyes, even "*the smallest leaf becomes a thing of wonder, and a blade of grass a sign of God's perfection*" (T-17.II.6:3). Everything is Divine and every delicate moment is precious, but it can only be seen through non-judgmental eyes.

> *Be present in the moment, where no guilty past abides, and no fearful future hides.*

The Past-Present Imperfect

The imperfect tense is a verb form which combines the past tense along with an imperfective aspect referencing a continuing or repeated event in the past—being described in the present as in "I used to walk." The Course, like Zen, teaches immediacy, immersion, and involvement, moment-to-moment. Zen says the mind is in the past. Guilt exists only in the present, if I hold on to it. Lesson 7 from the Workbook says, "*I see only the past.*"

> *Heaven is here. There is nowhere else. Heaven is now. There is no other time.*
> M-24.6: 4-7

Salvation is immediately available. We need not wait for a single second to enjoy it. Jesus in the Gospels says, "Heaven is at hand." It is as immediately available to me as my hand. When fully alive—there is no time for time.

The Path of Paradox

The Course says, "*All gifts I give my brothers are my own.*" (W.p.II.316.h). Zen says, "relax." 'on't seek, 'on't search, 'on't demand. Here is a secret. Seeking is unnecessary. Why go looking for what is already yours? If we can stop projecting the world, if we can relax, it comes. It does not come by demanding. It does not come through arrogance and it can never come by making others wrong. I wrote the following paragraphs one evening a couple of winters ago:

It's a winter evening and I'm sitting with my wife,
Dolores, and our daughter, Sarah, in our family room.
We're all reading. The fireplace is brightly ablaze. It feels
very comfy, very much like home—because it is home.

I stop reading and allow the moment to be what it is.
Here we are doing this essential family thing.

The moment is sufficient unto itself.
Nothing is needed.

This moment is perfect—just as it is. Right now reading
these words, the moment is perfect—just as it is.
And this morning when I was in a minor automobile
accident— that was perfect too.

Being Untethered

Being untethered to an ego, it is easy to live freely in the moment. Buddhist monks can laugh because they are free. When I was a kid on the farm in Missouri, we had a bull that even as a small child I could lead around with a rope. On one end of the rope there was a metal device with a spring on it that clasped around the soft inner part of the bull's nose between his two nostrils. If the bull pulled back on the rope, the metal clasp would tighten on the bull's nose. Stepping forward relieved the pressure. Thus, if I nudged on the rope, the bull would, in the most docile manner, follow me around. It's the same with the ego. The ego is a tether, a rope, a chain. It leads us around by our noses. What are you tethered to, a thought, an idea, an un-forgiveness, a hurt feeling?

> *If you can be hurt by anything, you see a picture of your secret wishes. Nothing more than this.*
>
> **T-31.V.15.8-9**

Egos are fragile and easily hurt. Have you ever said you are "upset," or "disappointed," or "disgusted," or "offended" because of what someone said? If so, you are buying into an illusion. Who is the "you" that can be hurt by an insult? If I can be hurt by words, I am not yet aware of Self. Of course the body can be hurt—but we are talking about the mind—only an ego can be hurt and—

YOU ARE NOT AN EGO!

Earth can reflect Heaven or hell; God or the ego.

T-14.IX.5:4

The Ego is Hell. There is No Other Hell.

"*The belief in hell is inescapable to those who identify with the ego*" (T-15.I.4:1). Zen says there is no ego. The Course says there is no ego. There is, thus, also no hell and no devil and nothing to be afraid of. There cannot be an opposite to that which is all-encompassing. There cannot be an opposite to the Eternal. Zen is just Being. The Course is just Being. And, there is no difference between Having and Being (T-4. VII.5:7).

> *The emphasis of the ego is on doing. The emphasis of Spirit is on being.*

I had a wonderful Zen-like experience in 2007 as a result of contracting viral La Crosse Encephalitis from a mosquito bite which put me in a coma for several days. After I awoke, I was not really back. I went so far down into black emptiness, I stopped thinking. After I awoke it took a long time before I could talk or even begin to do anything like what we call normal activity. It was incredibly peaceful, as I had none of the problems which plague normal consciousness. Slowly, slowly, over the course of many days, I began to regain control over my arms and legs and eventually my tongue. The thing that eventually brought me back was the thought, "You have bills to pay." It was almost as though I said, "Darn, you're back in the world again."

I thoroughly enjoy comparing the insights of the Course with the discoveries of the many mystics who experienced Holy Instances—those wonderful little glimpses into the truth that facilitate our awakening. Often these experiences come when we're not doing anything spectacular, when we just relax, or maybe if we're lucky, we actually stop thinking. Thus, I leave you with the writing of Douglas Harding (1909-2007) an English philosopher, mystic and spiritual teacher who wrote a wonderful book called *On Having No Head—Zen and the Rediscovery of the Obvious*. (For more information, go to www.headless.org.)

> *What actually happened was something absurdly simple and unspectacular: I stopped thinking. A peculiar quiet, an odd kind of alert limpness or numbness, came over me. Reason and imagination and all mental chatter died down. For once, words*

really failed me. Past and future dropped away. I forgot who and what I was, my name, manhood, animalhood, all that could be called mine. It was as if I had been born that instant, brand new, mindless, innocent of all memories. There existed only the Now, that present moment and what was clearly given in it. To look was enough. And what I found was khaki trouser legs terminating downwards in a pair of brown shoes, khaki sleeves terminating sideways in a pair of pink hands, and a khaki shirtfront terminating upwards in—absolutely nothing hatever! Certainly not in a head!

Jon Mundy, Ph.D. is an author, lecturer, the publisher of *Miracles* magazine and the Executive Director of All Faiths Seminary International in New York City. He taught university courses in philosophy from 1967 to 2008. The author of 11 books his earlier book, *Living A Course in Miracles* has become a perennial best-seller and now exists in 8 languages. He has also produced over 100 YouTube presentations. Jon met Dr. Helen Schucman the scribe of *A Course in Miracles* in 1973. Helen introduced Jon to the Course and served as his counselor till she became ill in 1980. He also appears on occasion as *Dr. Baba Jon Mundane*, a standup philosopher comedian. jon@miraclesmagazine.org

Section II

Western Religious Teachings

Chapter 7

Judaism

Dr. Bob Rosenthal

A Course in Miracles tells us many times in many different ways that there is only one truth and that "*the truth is true, and nothing else is true*" (W-pI.152.3:1) Nor can truth be completely suppressed by the ego's dream of separation. "*Truth is not absent here, but it is obscure*" (T-11.VII.4:5). It is not absent because it is our essential nature. If *we* are here, then so is truth; so is love. They cannot help but shine through the illusion in some fashion.

The Course also tells us that its teaching is but one of "many thousands" of forms of the "universal course" (M-1.4:1-2), all of which lead to truth. In a dream world of myriad forms, this is hardly surprising and perhaps even necessary. What speaks to one particular person, culture or time period may be anathema to another. Therefore, we should be able to find truth in all of the world's great religions. This is not always easy, however, because the ego prefers laws and rituals over love and forgiveness. It cherishes form over substance, the frame over the picture. Thus, the world's religions are fraught with rules—the thou-shalts and shalt-nots—that tell us how we should live within the illusion rather than how to escape from it. The result is more guilt, more fear, and more judgment; leading to confusion at best and blind obedience or righteous attack at worst.

To extract the truth in a spiritual teaching from the fearful ego-imposed rules, we need to know how to look. We need to be able to discern truth no matter the form in which it may appear—to recognize the luster of true gold shimmering within the heaps of worthless dross. The Course helps us to do this. The consistency and purity of its message teaches us to recognize other true teachings, no matter their form. Truth is truth, whether clothed in the garb and traditions of Islam, Shinto, Zen, or Shamanism.

Rarely, however, do the leaders of different religious traditions welcome the idea of a universal truth underlying all religions. The

German mystic Meister Eckhart was excommunicated for proclaiming this truth. The Islamic Sufi, al-Hallaj, was beheaded. Jesus' original teachings were all too often misunderstood and distorted by his followers, as the Course itself points out (T-6.I.14:2-16:1).

By contrast, the Course's parallels with Eastern religions are fairly easy to spot. Buddhism enjoins us to cultivate compassion when confronted with a world of *dukkha* (dissatisfaction, suffering). Is this not simply another way of expressing forgiveness? One of the Course's scribes, Bill Thetford, liked to describe the Course as "the Christian Vedanta," that is, Christian in its language, but espousing a non-dual philosophy identical to that of the Upanishads of Vedanta Hinduism.

But what about Judaism? Jesus was himself a Jew. We could rightly expect that his teachings in the Course would in some way mirror the religion in which he was raised. And yet, the correspondences between the Course and Judaism are not all that obvious, for the very reasons discussed above.

There are, in fact, two cornerstones of Judaism which closely parallel the teachings of the Course. The first of these is the story of Exodus—but only if we view it as parable, not history. I have explored this idea at length in my book, *From Plagues to Miracles: The Transformational Journey of Exodus, From the Slavery of Ego to the Promised Land of Spirit*, so I will only touch on it briefly here. In Exodus, we who have lost our way in deserts of illusion are represented by the Hebrew people.

(The word for "Hebrew" in the Hebrew language is *ivrit*, and it originally meant nomad or wanderer.) The characters of Moses and Pharaoh represent dueling aspects of our mind, vying for our allegiance. Moses is the embodiment of our eternal, unshakeable oneness with God, that is, Christ and Holy Spirit in Course terms. Pharaoh is the ego: a slave master inflicting suffering, intent on maintaining power and control; a bully who vacillates between arrogant contempt and pathetic false promises; an entity that denies God and His miracles while posing as God's equal. According to this interpretation, Exodus becomes a chronicle of our journey back to God—to the real world, the Promised Land.

There is a second aspect of Judaism that more directly reflects the Course's teaching. This is the Kabbalistic doctrine of *Tikkun Olam*: the repair or healing of the world. The tale behind *tikkun olam* relates yet another version of the separation or the Fall, and it goes as follows. In order to create the world, God poured the essence of His Being into a vessel of light. But the vessel shattered, fragmenting God's creation into countless shards of light, all now separate and bound within the world of physical matter—that is, the ego's world of form. Those splintered shards are *us*. And so, according to this understanding, it becomes the duty of each one of us to help repair the fracture by reuniting the broken and scattered shards back into the oneness that God intended. This process of repair (or healing) is called *tikkun olam*. Thus, *tikkun olam* is the equivalent of the Course's idea of Atonement.

Notice how closely this tracks with the Course:

> *It should especially be noted that God has only* one *Son. If all His creations are His Sons, every one must be an integral part of the whole Sonship. The Sonship in its oneness transcends the sum of its parts. However, this is obscured as long as any of its parts is missing. That is why the conflict cannot ultimately be resolved until all the parts of the Sonship have returned. The correction of this error is the Atonement.*
>
> **T-2.VII.6:1-5, 9**

> *What is the world except a little gap perceived to tear eternity apart, and break it into days and months and years? And what are you who live within the world except a picture of the Son of God in broken pieces, each concealed within a separate and uncertain bit of clay?*
>
> **T-28.III.7:4-5**

> *You who believe that God is fear made but one substitution ... the substitution of illusion for truth; of fragmentation for wholeness. It has become so splintered and subdivided and divided again, over and over, that it is now almost impossible to perceive it once was one, and still is what it was. That one error ... was all you ever made.... But nothing you have seen begins to show you the enormity of the original error, which seemed to cast you out of Heaven,*

to shatter knowledge into meaningless bits of disunited perceptions, and to force you to make further substitutions.

T-18.I.4:1-4; 5:6

Of course, it is not God who fumbled and shattered the light of His wholeness into separate parts; it was us. In this respect, the Course corrects a misunderstanding of Kabbalah—that for some unfathomable reason God chose to hide His Light from us. In God's Reality, none of this ever even occurred; only in the ongoing fever-dream of time and materiality does God's Son perceive His oneness to be fractured. The ego peers through its insane kaleidoscope of sin and guilt to behold a chaotic world of separate bodies, private minds, and distinct physical objects, all appearing to exist independently outside of us.

Judaism envisions the healing work of *tikkun olam* as an external process. We repair the fractured parts by performing good deeds out in the world. But as students of the Course we know there *is* no external world. It is the projection of our own mind: an effect, not a cause. Any attempt to take action at the level of the effect, however well-intentioned, must be limited in its impact. It cannot heal the split Sonship. Worse still, when we focus on healing the effect, it reinforces for us its seeming reality. We continue to believe that it is the world that's in need of healing, rather than our minds. The real healing of the fragmentation of God's Son can only take place internally, in the mind that is the source of the projection.

And here, fortunately, we have help. God created the Holy Spirit and placed Him within the mind of God's Son specifically to bring about this healing and repair.

The Holy Spirit's function is to take the broken picture of the Son of God and put the pieces into place again. To each [separate piece] He offers his Identity, which the whole picture represents, instead of just a little, broken bit that he insisted was himself. And when he sees this picture, he will recognize himself.

T-28.IV.8:1, 3-4

How then do we perform our part in *tikkun olam*? How do we fuse the seemingly separate, divided aspects of the Sonship back into oneness? It is not enough to do good deeds. It is not enough to pray for others. It is not enough to seek God on your own terms, in your own private sanctuary. Unless you learn to perceive the holy light of God within *everyone* (thereby acknowledging that same light in yourself), you are maintaining the illusion of separation. And here lies the true meaning of *tikkun olam*: to see the light of God shining through the façade of a fractured, separate, ego-body self such that any sense of separateness dissolves away and oneness is again remembered.

The Course calls this Christ's Vision. Another name for it is forgiveness, yet another, the Atonement. "*Though every aspect* is *the whole, you cannot know this until you see that every aspect is the same, perceived in the same light and therefore one*" (T-13.VIII.5:3). When we can finally look upon all our brothers as one, identical to us, sharing the same Self, then we have repaired the fracture and the work of *tikkun olam* is complete.

Robert Rosenthal, M.D., is the author of *From Plagues to Miracles: The Transformational Journey of Exodus, From the Slavery of Ego to the Promised Land of Spirit*. He was a protégé of Bill Thetford, one of the scribes of the Course, and has served on the Board of the Foundation for Inner Peace since 1992. He is currently Co-President of the Foundation for Inner Peace. DrBob@acim.org

Chapter 8

The Kabbalah

Bonnie Nack, Ed.D.

The Kabbalah literally means "receiving." The Kabbalah is a 2000-year-old system of thought that is concerned with the mystical aspect of Judaism. It therefore relies upon classical Jewish sources and vocabulary. For most of its existence the Kabbalah was "hidden knowledge," and kept secret until modern times. It is practically unknown in some denominations of Judaism and heavily relied upon in others. It seeks to define the nature of the universe and the human being and the purpose of existence. It provides methods and disciplines to aid in the understanding of its concepts. The goal of a student of the Kabbalah is the attainment of a fulfilling life and firsthand Knowledge of God. Firsthand knowledge of God is achieved by what is termed "Dvekut" or "Adhesion."

A Course in Miracles was also "received" by its scribe, Helen Schucman. It is a system of thought developed during the twentieth century using Christian symbolism but within the realm of psychology; therefore its vocabulary and sources rely heavily upon those two systems of thought. The Course defines the nature of the universe and the nature of human beings and provides methods and disciplines to aid the student to understand its concepts. Its goal is the attainment of a fulfilling life and firsthand Knowledge of God. Firsthand knowledge of God is achieved by what is termed "Atonement." (It seems that there is nothing new under the sun after all.)

This article looks at just a few basic principles of the Kabbalah that are similar to that of the Course. It will be seen that although the form of the two paths to God are very different, with some seeming contradictions, in essence they are the same. I have been studying the Course seriously for about six years, and the Kabbalah for only six months. But learning about this ancient system of thought has greatly strengthened my faith in, and deepened my understanding of, the more modern Course. Within my limited understanding of both disciplines,

I feel competent to discuss one Kabbalistic lesson and compare it with the teachings of the Course: "Make for Yourself a Rav and Buy for Yourself a Friend."

In order that the reader can get the flavor of the way Kabbalah is taught, I will quote from a textbook, "The Social Writings" by Rabash, (a modern writer who provided the link connecting the Wisdom of Kabbalah to our human experience). Remember that we are learning here from sources that are over two-thousand-years old.

"In the Mishnah, (the first written form of oral teachings) it is written: "Make for yourself a rav, buy yourself a friend, and judge every person favorably." We see there are three things here: 1) Make for yourself a rav; 2) buy yourself a friend; 3) judge every person favorably" (P.68 Rabash). A rav is a great spiritual teacher.

"We should interpret "make" as "excluding from reason." This is because when reason cannot understand if something is worth doing, how can it determine what is good for me? Or vice versa, if reason considers them equal, who will determine for a person what he should do? Thus, the act can decide (P.77, Rabash). The results from doing the act will help reason decide what to do.

"Therefore, (without understanding why) the order of the work is for one to begin with "Make for yourself a rav," (a great teacher) and take upon himself the burden of the kingdom of heaven above logic and above reason. This is called "doing," meaning action only, despite the body's disapproval. Afterwards, "Buy yourself a friend." Buying means when a person wishes to buy something; he must let go of something that he has already acquired. He gives what he's had for some time and in return purchases a new object" (P.69, Rabash).

"It is similar with the work of God. For one to achieve Dvekut (Adhesion) with the Creator, which is equivalence of form, as in, "As He is merciful, you be merciful, too," he must concede many things that he has in order to buy bonding with the Creator. This is the meaning of "Buy yourself a friend." (p. 69, Rabash).

The word "favorably" implies differences in evaluating people. Reason teaches that some people are more favorable than others. "Judge every person favorably means that with regards to the rest of the people (those who are deemed less favorable) he should go above reason" (P.82

Rabash). "… he should judge them favorably and say that they truly are more important people than himself, and that it is his own fault that he cannot appreciate the greatness and importance of the public, called by our sages, 'every person'" (P82, Rabash).

The Kabbalists express themselves in even more obtuse form than does Jesus in the Course. It takes time to study and understand the language of both the Kabbalah and the Course.

I will try to make it easy. The three concepts—making a rav, buying a friend and judging each person favorably—are functionally related with each other. We can summarize these Kabbalistic teachings as follows: It is against what is called common sense to judge every person favorably. The Kabbalists say you have to make yourself do it, even if it does not make sense to your reason, like an ox takes on the yoke unwillingly to get the job done. The Kabbalists teach that this kind of relationship to our brother is against human nature. But it is precisely in going against the dictates of the ego or nature that atonement or adhesion with God is achieved. Both disciplines also call upon a higher spiritual force to accomplish the goal of transcending nature or the ego.

But the only way you can judge another person favorably is to give up negative judgments about him. That is "buying" a friend in Kabbalists terms. The price of a holy relationship with a brother or friend is giving up something you have (judgments) in order to get something you want. What you want is adhesion with God. According to the Kabbalists, by thinking well of your friend you thereby "buy" your bond to the Creator. Your friend then becomes your "rav" or great teacher.

In Kabalistic writing the word "make" is interpreted to mean "coming to exclude from reason." This is because if reason cannot determine if something is good for me or not, how can I determine what is good for me?" The inadequacy of reason in spiritual matters is discussed in the Course as well: "*Babies scream in rage if you take away a knife or scissors, although they may well harm themselves if you do not. In this sense you are still a baby. You have no sense of real self-preservation, and are likely to decide that you need precisely what would hurt you most*" (T-4 II.5:2-4). Therefore, both disciplines teach that in matters of spirituality people cannot make judgments about what is good or right for them to do.

The Course teaches that your brother is your savior when you forgive him. We could equate the word "rav" with "savior." Both words refer to teachers whose goal is to lift you out of the thought system of this world. The Kabbalah and the Course both teach that your brother or friend is your greatest spiritual teacher—but only under one condition: that you don't judge him and that you think only good of him. To think only good of someone is the equivalent to not condemning them. The Course teaches that we should not condemn our brother because without condemnation even forgiveness is not needed.

The Kabbalah teaches you should go even further than that. Not only should you think well of your friend, you should tell yourself it is your own fault that you cannot appreciate the greatness and importance of your brother and by extension all people. The Course teaches the same principle in a different form. When we achieve Vision, (spiritual sight) we will see Christ in everyone. So indeed Kabbalists are correct when they say it is our own fault we do not see the greatness and importance of our brothers.

In the Course, Jesus teaches: "*Today I learn the law of love; that what I give my brother is my gift to myself*" (W-p.II.344.h). "*By attacking nothing, He (the Holy Spirit) presents no barrier to communication from God*" (T6 III 1:4). This is the great secret that is taught in both in the Course and the Kabbalah: When you give up judgment of your brother (attack thoughts) and see only the highest in him you become more like God, and that leads you ultimately to Atonement or Adhesion.

The Course teaches: "*God gave you and your brother Himself, and to remember this is now the only purpose that you share. And so it is the only one you have*" (T-24.I.7:5-6). Both the Course and the Kabbalah teach that the only purpose for which you have been given life is to find your way back to the Creator or God. Devkut or Adhesion are functionally the same as Atonement: both refer to being like God in order to become one with Him. The Course teaches the holiest spot on earth is the place where an ancient hatred has been changed to love. In the words of the Zohar (The Book of Wisdom of the Kabbalah), finding unity with your brother is called "Raising Divinity from the dust," which means raising the kingdom of heaven, which is lowered into the dust (p. 71 Rabash).

Both the Kabbalah and the Course teach that the doorway to heaven, knowing God and who we really are—will not open until we learn to love our brother as ourselves.

The wording of both the Course and the Kabalistic writings at first seems obscure and difficult to understand. Both reveal their meaning gradually and only with study and practice of the principles taught. When the meaning is revealed to the student, he realizes that the obscure wording reached him at a deeper level than more obvious presentations of the same ideas. Somehow when the obscure language releases its meaning to us, it awakens a memory in our hearts of Truth, placed there by God when He created us.

Because the essence of the Course is supported by the 2000-year-old teachings of the Kabbalah, my faith in the process of finding my way back home to God via the Course is strengthened. I love the quote from the Course about faith: "*And with Him, you will build a ladder planted in the solid rock of faith, and rising even to Heaven*" (T-18.V.2:7). Most especially I like the phrase: "*the solid rock of faith.*" Who would ever think that faith—something the Kabbalists would say is above reason, and the Course would say is without form—could become as solid as a rock?

Bonnie Nack, Ed.D. is a retired psychologist who worked for 25 years in community mental health; the mother of two daughters and grandmother of three grandsons. She is the author of *Twelve Keys to Unlocking the Secret of Miracles in A Course in Miracles.* She is presently working on another book; a *User's Manual* for souls who find themselves in human bodies. BonnieNack99@gmail.com

Chapter 9

Jesus' Biblical Teachings

Harry McDonald

How does what Jesus reportedly taught in the Bible compare with what he teaches in *A Course in Miracles*? First it needs to be identified what he taught in the Bible and the circumstances surrounding the recording of those teachings. It is assumed that the New Testament is consistent in what is taught about Jesus' teachings, but that is not the case. That is especially true when looking at translations, audiences, and interpretations through the centuries. Bible scholars have made many important discoveries in the past half century that shed light on the sources and ages of texts in the New Testament.

For purposes of this short article, where brevity is important, the considerations will be narrowed to the Gospels, especially Matthew, Luke, and Mark that are commonly called the synoptic Gospels, or "seen through one eye." The reason the synoptic Gospels are chosen is that the writings of Paul, though written earlier than the synoptics, were reflective of a man who did not know Jesus personally, but had a significant spiritual experience of him. The Gospel of John, though very beautiful, is reflective of a more fully developed theology than the synoptics and, according to most scholars, is a later creation. Other early sources, like the book of Thomas, are obviously outside the scope of an article about the Bible.

The earliest synoptic Gospel, Mark, is also the shortest and the simplest. It was likely written in Rome just before the fall of Jerusalem to the Romans in 70 AD, but not "published" until after the fall. It does not include a virgin birth story or a resurrection story except as added later. It has a climax in the suffering and crucifixion. It does not outline a doctrine per se, but is more interested in establishing Jesus as Messiah and Son of God, which is problematic without a virgin birth. Mark's main importance for this article is that it was a source for both Matthew and Luke.

Matthew also used material from a lost sayings document or

tradition designated "Q" by scholars and in special traditions, designated "M." Matthew seems to be written to Jews. Luke was written a little later to Greeks to show Jesus as a universal savior. The author of Luke was also the author of Acts. Much of what is related in Matthew is also in Luke, but Luke also has some unique stories. The major section of Matthew that gives teachings is the Sermon on the Mount section, and in Luke the parallel is the Sermon on the Plain section.

The contrasts in the subtleties of these two sections could be a whole article, but here are some ideas about Jesus' teachings: The Beatitudes sections rejoice at a state where those who are hurt, poor or falsely accused will receive blessings. Luke says that the rich and full have already had their reward (6:24). In fact, Luke in general even sends woe to those who are well thought of instead of falsely accused (6:26). Both Matthew and Mark state to love your enemies, not to resist evildoers, turn the other cheek, give more than is asked to accusers, do not judge others, etc. (Matt. 5:33-46, Luke 6:27-37). The Golden Rule is also espoused by both (Matt. 7:12, Luke 6:31).

Matthew seems to talk about what the Course calls projection, in that Jesus is reported to say that if you get angry with a brother you will be liable to judgment, with insults getting even more of a consequence (5:22-26). There is a line in the Lord's Prayer from both Matthew and Luke that says, "Forgive us our debts as we have forgiven our debtors," (or trespasses or sins) that demonstrates the necessity of forgiving what we have projected onto others (Matt. 6:12, Luke 11:4).

Both Matthew and Luke say that we cannot serve both Heaven and the world, that we should take no thought for clothes or food, and that by choosing God all other things are added unto us (Matt. 6:19-34, Luke 12:22-34). Luke and Matthew both say that we are recognized by the good in our heart that causes good works. Matthew goes so far as to say that Jesus will not recognize those who cast out demons or prophesied in his name or did other deeds of power unless they did good deeds from a heart that values God over the world (Matt 7:15-23, Luke 6:43-46). Mark did not contribute to any of these major points except for the Lord's Prayer (11:25-26) and judgment (4:24-25). John, written much later, did not include any of these references.

Luke and Matthew's inclusion of earlier sources could come from eye witnesses, even though both Gospels were written after the fall of Jerusalem some 40 to 50 years or more after the crucifixion. Most of these citations also carry a promise of punishment. It is not always clear whether the punishment is a natural result of those actions or will be done by God. The actual message could also have been corrupted by followers, given its later date, who wanted to put more teeth in it to keep followers in line during times of persecution and torture.

The parallels with the Course are striking, except modern psychological terms are used in the Course. Further, there would never be a reference of a punishing God. God in the Course is loving and steadfast while it is we who have made a choice to think apart from God and make illusions that can never endanger reality. Also, the Course never demonizes being wealthy, but it does say not to put our faith in money, medicines, food, or earthly things. The admonition to take no thought for what is worn or eaten could be considered a way of giving the ego less power and turning all guidance over to the Holy Spirit.

> *You think you must obey the "laws" of medicine, of economics and of health. Protect the body and you will be saved. These are not laws, but madness.*
>
> W-P.I.76:4:3-4; 5:1

> *Dismiss all foolish magical beliefs today, and hold your mind in silent readiness to hear the Voice that speaks the truth to you. You will be listening to One Who says there is no loss under the laws of God.*
>
> W-P.I.76:9:2-3

Jesus says he will make all small decisions for us, if we allow it, with his guidance influencing our big decisions.

> *My control can take over everything that does not matter, while my guidance can direct everything that does, if you so choose.*
>
> T-2:VI.1:3

The preferred way in the Course is for us to be the hands and feet of Christ (lesson #353) and turn actions over to the direction of the Holy Spirit. The Bible's "seek first the kingdom of Heaven" idea is mirrored in lesson 151 and also the twin lessons of 128 & 129. These sections and others state that our earthly desires are false solutions to grief caused by our separation from God. The correction is to seek God so that all our reasonable needs are met automatically.

My eyes, my tongue, my hands, my feet today
Have but one purpose; to be given Christ
To use to bless the world with miracles.

W-P.II.353

The world you see holds nothing that you need to offer you; nothing that you can use in any way, nor anything at all that serves to give you joy.

W-P.I.128.1:1

Beyond this world there is a world I want...
Our emphasis is not on giving up the world, but on exchanging it for what is far more satisfying, filled with joy, and capable of offering you peace.

W-P.I.129...1:3

The biblical admonitions about good works needing to come from the pure heart rather than personal "power" are not widely recognized as major concepts in the Course, but they are there. The early encouragement to *listen, learn, and do* is part of Jesus' great crusade, and expresses that actions should be the result of listening and learning from Jesus' guidance. Most teachers of ACIM agree that the emphasis of ACIM is on forgiveness. However, not as many emphasize that forgiveness requires *acting* from a loving center that reflects God's unconditional love. Hence, miracles are involuntary, automatic responses, while consciously selected miracles are seen as misguided.

As you share my unwillingness to accept error in yourself and others, you must join the great crusade to correct it; listen to my voice, learn to undo error and act to correct it.

T-1.III.1:6

> *Miracles are habits and should be involuntary. They should not be under conscious control. Consciously selected miracles can be misguided.*
>
> **MIRACLE PRINCIPLE #5, T-1.I.5**

The major biblical ideas of non-judgment, forgiveness, and a spiritual reality, Heaven, which is separate from this world, are the same thoughts that Jesus uses in the Course with modern terms. The crucifixion seems to be the supreme example of turning the other cheek and loving your enemies while the resurrection is the triumph of God's love over adversity and even death. They become the glowing picture of putting faith in the energy of God's unconditional love (Heaven) over this world. In the Course, however, we are now told that it is no longer necessary for us to participate in useless journeys.

> *Do not embark on useless journeys, because they are indeed in vain. The journey to the cross should be the last "useless journey." Do not dwell upon it, but dismiss it as accomplished. If you can accept it as your own last useless journey, you are also free to join my resurrection. The only message of the crucifixion is that you can overcome the cross.*
>
> **T-4.IN.2:5; 3:1-3, 8**

In the Bible, when asked how long one should forgive, Jesus told his followers "seventy times seven" (Matt. 18:22). In the Course, the forgiveness we are asked to practice relies on miracles and Divine direction. Nor can we forgive without actually giving God's unconditional love to each other.

> *Forgiveness recognizes what you thought your brother did to you has not occurred. It does not pardon sins and make them real. It sees there was no sin.*
>
> **W-P.II.1.1:1-3**

> *Do nothing, then, and let forgiveness show you what to do, through Him Who is your Guide, your Savior and Protector...*
>
> **W-P.II.1.5:1**

In conclusion, what Jesus taught as a man in the earliest sources in the Gospels certainly appears the same as what he teaches in the Course, once the inconsistency of unloving punishment is brushed off like later-added rust from a strongly loving message.

Harry McDonald was a Licensed School Counselor and Licensed Professional Counselor. He and his wife, Janie, worked in Montrose, CO for thirty years. He is now retired, living in Grand Junction, Colorado, and has taught *A Course in Miracles* since 1985. He is the author of many articles for *Miracles Magazine* and the novel *Touched by Love.* He currently teaches *A Course in Miracles* in Grand Junction, CO. He can be reached via email at harry.mcdonald1@gmail.com

Chapter 10

Sufism

DJ Andrews

Remembering the Beloved

A Sufi story tells of a young girl on her way to see her beloved. She passed by a Mullah (holy man) who was saying his prayers. In her ignorance, she walked in front of him, which was forbidden by the religious law. The Mullah, his prayers having been disturbed, became upset. Later, upon returning, she again passed near him. He scolded her for her mistake saying, "It was not right for you to cross in front of me while I was offering my prayer. I was thinking of God, the Lord of heaven and earth." She replied, "I'm sorry. I don't know yet of God and His prayers. I was on the way to see my beloved and, thinking of my beloved, I did not see you praying. I wonder how you, who were thinking of God, could see me?"

Sufism, by its nature, tends to elude definition. The word *Sufism* is variously traced to an Arabic source (*Saaf*) which means "purity" or to the Greek "sophos," meaning wisdom. Inayat Khan, bringer of Sufism to the West in 1910, describes Sufism as a path of the heart, a path of love, and a path of oneness.

Although of ancient origins, pre-dating Islam, Sufism is also an active, contemporary path. The Sufi Ruhaniat International (the Way of the Breath) is one of a dozen or so Sufi Orders in the United States. This Order draws inspiration from the roots, branches, and flowers of Sufism within and beyond historic Islam. *Ruh* is spirit or breath of God, thus, this is a path of remembering God with every breath.

This article reflects an experience of association with the Sufi Ruhaniat International and *A Course in Miracles*. Both paths will speak in their own voices throughout to convey the flavor of the experience. It was the mystical poet, Kabir, who said, "Kabir talks only about what he has lived through. If you have not lived through something, it is not true."

Sufism is not a path of a book and is primarily an oral tradition, "based on experiences, not premises," according to Al-Ghazali, a prominent Sufi mystic. There is no text to reference, per se, though some study the Qur'an. It is more about a *way* of living, a way of being in the world but not of it. This concept is exemplified in the Course when it talks of living within this world of illusion, the world of separate bodies, but learning to see with the vision of Christ, seeing with *true perception*, and as the Sufi poet, Rumi, suggested, "seeing One with two eyes." Then God takes the last step Himself, and that is what finally awakens us from the dream entirely (T-11.VIII.15:5). We then experience, as the Sufi would say, union with the Beloved.

What Are We Remembering?

Ibn Hasan told of prophets who were sent to encourage people to say "Allah" and devote themselves to Him. Those who heard this word with the ear alone let it go out by the other ear; but those who heard it with their *souls*, imprinted it on their souls and repeated it until it penetrated their hearts and souls, and their whole being *became* this word. They were released from the sound and the letters. Having come to experience the spiritual meaning of this word, they became so absorbed in it that they were no longer conscious of their own non-existence (no longer focused on the self, small "s").

Inayat Khan writes that the main ideal of all Sufi schools has been to attain that perfection which Jesus taught in the Bible, "Be ye perfect as your Father in Heaven is perfect" (Matthew 5:48), and that the method of the Sufis has always been self-effacement. This effacement is "of the false self, on which man depends, priding himself on being something, but not of the real self which is eternal, and to which all power and beauty belong." The Course, too, reminds us:

> *The Bible enjoins you to be perfect, to heal all errors, to take no thought of the body as separate and to accomplish all things in my name.*
> T-8.IX.7:1.

The Course invites us multiple times to repeat the Name of God and reminds us that:

> *To call upon His Name is but to call upon your own God has no name. And yet His Name becomes the final*

lesson that all things are one, and at this lesson does all learning end. Experience must come to supplement the Word. But first you must accept the Name for all reality. One Name we use to unify our sight.

W-P.I.183.1:2; 184.12:1-2; 13:2-3,5

*Love created me like itself (and) perfection created me perfect. If love created you like itself, this Self must be in you. And somewhere in your mind (*not to be confused with the physical brain*) It is there for you to find.*

W.P.I.67:H; 2:6; 3:2-3

How We Remember

"Know that when you learn to lose yourself (your self), you will reach the Beloved. There is no other secret to be learned" (Al-Ansari). In Sufism, one aid to remembering God or recovering our memory of Unity is simply the repetition of the name of God, referred to as *Allah* in the Middle East, originally meaning *the Source, the Oneness.* A more extended form of this remembrance, a practice called *zikr*, uses the words *la illaha illa'llah.* ("There is no god but God," or "There is no reality except the One Reality.") One can Remember silently, in chant, song, music, movement, or in dance form.

The learning goal of the Course is summed up in the introduction which says that this curriculum aims at "*...removing the blocks to the awareness of love's presence, which is your natural inheritance*" (T-in.1:7). The method of learning includes study of the Text, which guides one through a psychological process, and application of the suggestions that appear throughout the Text and within the 365 Workbook practice lessons.

Seek ye first the Kingdom of Heaven. There is *nothing else. By your awakening to (love), you are merely forgetting what you are not. This enables you to remember what you are.*

(T-7.IV.7:1,3,11-12).

Lesson 122 says forgiveness is the answer:

> *It lets you recognize the Son of God, and clears your memory of all dead thoughts so that remembrance of our Father can arise across the threshold of your mind.*
>
> W-P.I.122.3:2

Forgiveness acknowledges that, in Truth, the error never occurred; therefore, only we can deprive ourselves of the peace of God. The importance and nature of forgiveness is echoed by these words of Inayat Khan: "If you wish to follow the path of saints, learn to forgive," and "Forgiveness is a stream of love which washes away all impurities wherever it flows." Although the Workbook exercises are intended to be experiential, Lesson 158 reminds us that:

> *Experience cannot be shared directly... The revelation that the Father and the Son are one will come in time to every mind. Yet is that time determined by the mind itself, not taught.*
>
> W-P.I.158.2:7-9

The closing section of the Workbook leads us to seek direct experience of truth and come to beingness.

One day as Rumi was instructing a group of students, Shams-i-Tabriz, his close companion and teacher, suddenly took Rumi's books and threw them into the pond, announcing, "You must live what you know!"

The Sufi way embraces both silent and active forms of meditation, breathing practices, and guidance through the teacher-student dynamic. Inayat Khan comments that saying words aloud reaches to the inner plane of one's being, and action makes pictures in every atom of the body of the thought which is behind it. Every atom of the body prays. The whole being becomes a prayer.

Some new work with meditation, based on traditional methods, has been published by Neil Douglas-Klotz, a Sufi teacher and Aramaic scholar. It includes breath, sound, and movement practices based on translations of Jesus' sayings from his native Aramaic language. Likewise, the Dances of Universal Peace are a form of movement meditation originally developed by Samuel L. Lewis, a student of Inayat Khan and founder of the Sufi Ruhaniat International. Samuel Lewis once said, "One of the reasons I am teaching this music and dancing is to increase Joy…bliss in our own self (Self). This is finding God within, through Experience." The lyrics of one such Dance, taken from Shabistari's *Rose Garden of Mystery*, present a traditional Middle-Eastern image of how we remember. He writes, "Go sweep out the chambers of your heart. Make it ready to be the dwelling of the Beloved. When you depart, love will enter. In you, void of yourself (your self), God will display His beauties."

Another image found in Sufi poetry is that of wiping rust from a mirror. This image also appears in the Course:

> *Clean but the mirror, and the message that shines forth from what the mirror holds out for everyone to see, no one can fail to understand.*
>
> T-14.IX.6:5

The Sufi guide assists with this purification and healing process. With the help of this friend on the path, the student can observe and better "catch" the teachings in action. One comes then to living inwardly in the manner of the teacher (tasawwuri), one of the defining practices of the Sufi way. This relationship is mutually interactive. "Very often a student is an inspiration for the teacher because it is not the teacher who teaches, it is God Himself" (Inayat Khan).

In the Course, both Jesus and the Holy Spirit serve as our inner teachers. Jesus, in the Text says,

> *Healing does not come from anyone else. You must accept guidance from within…healing is a collaborative venture. I can tell you what to do, but you must collaborate by believing that I know what you should do. One Teacher is in all minds and He teaches the same lesson to all.*
>
> *(The Holy Spirit) is in your mind and...He is helping you to remember what you are.*
>
> T-8.IV.4:5-9; T-7.VII.7:2; T-9.I.4:3-4

Inayat Khan writes, "The Spirit of Guidance (the Holy Spirit) is the light of God which may be likened to a search light which shows up any object upon which it is thrown, and so when (this light) is thrown upon any aspect of life, man receives a keen insight into it. In the Spirit of Guidance one finds a living God, active in the heart of every person…One who depends upon the Spirit of Guidance to direct his life is guided rightly."

Fruits of Remembrance

In Sufism, signs of progress on the spiritual path include: inspiration, power, joy, fearlessness, and peace. In reference to Jesus' words in the Bible: "Let your light so shine before all men, that they may see your good works, and glorify your Father which is in heaven" (Matthew 5:16), Neil Douglas-Klotz comments, "Hearing this blessing of permission with Aramaic ears, we find Yeshua (Jesus) showing what happens when the light of our being—a tangible sense of our personal 'I am'—connects to the sacred 'I Am' and allows itself to shine. First, we bless those around us by reminding them subconsciously that there is a greater reality to which we are all connected. Second, we bless our own inner self, the inner community of voices called the 'naphsha' in Aramaic and 'nafs' in Arabic…(allowing) these voices 'in the shadow' to be illuminated and feel a more expanded, connected sense of divine Self."

The Course teaches, *"When I have forgiven myself and remembered Who I am, I will bless everyone and everything I see"* (W-p.I.52.2:5), and affirms that God's messengers are joyous and peaceful. The path to the Beloved may lead one to discover that *"You who are beloved of God are wholly blessed"* (T-8.VI.10:4).

> *In you is all of Heaven. Every leaf that falls is given life in you. Each bird that ever sang will sing again in you. And every flower that ever bloomed has saved its perfume and its loveliness for you…*
>
> *This can you bring to all the world.*
>
> **T-25.IV.5:1-4, 11**

Although there are differences in form between these two spiritual paths, both *A Course in Miracles* and Sufism share the same content, which is Love.

DJ Andrews is *A Course in Miracles* and a Ruhaniat' student, has a Master's degree in Addiction Studies, and lives in Peoria, IL where she is a counselor at a drug treatment program. She completed leadership certification training for the Dances of Universal Peace and published a monograph, *Knowing Peace and Changing Outlooks: Weaving the Dances of Universal Peace into Medical and Behavioral Treatment Models for Substance Abuse*. djandrews1001@gmail.com

Chapter 11

Sufism

Clarice O'Bryan

Sufism, as well as *A Course in Miracles*, calls one to remember the true Self, to remember that one has never left Home. Both are inclusive in the sense that both teach that all people are one and that all religions contain perennial wisdom. The ways of answering the summons may differ in that Sufism is mostly handed down by word of mouth through prophets and enlightened teachers whereas the three volumes of the Course were channeled from an enlightened teacher, Jesus the Christ.

It is my understanding that the ultimate rebirthing in this world is experienced only after one has experienced oneself as pure spirit. Nevertheless, 1977 was a year of rebirthing for me. I was at the lowest point of my life when I was introduced to both Sufism and the Course. Each appeared to be coincidental but of course we know nothing truly is.

A spiritual teacher confidentially whispered to me that if I wanted to go deeper I should check out the Course. I ordered my books the same day. The next month, I attended a metaphysical seminar and heard the Sufis drumming in another room. The drums called to my soul and I answered. For several years I attended a Sufi summer camp in North Carolina led by Adnan Sarhan, and four years later was initiated into the Sufi order by the head of the Sufi Order of the West, Pir Vilayat Inayat Khan.

Both the Course and Sufism invited me to go within. Both offered me the experience of feeling the presence of God. As I dedicated my self to the Course and whirled with the Dervishes I experienced deeper and deeper revelations.

Hazrat Inayat Khan, who was Pir Vilayat Inayat Khan's father, planted the seeds of the ancient wisdom of the Sufis in the West in 1910. As with all seeds that are transplanted to new soil, so it is with all cultures, spiritual traditions, and teachings. New, often-unexpected hybrids and a multiplicity of varieties and forms flower. This is true of Sufism as well as Christianity. There are different Sufi sects that transfer the teachings in different ways. Whereas the Course community does not consider itself an organization, Hazrat found it necessary to "have a basket for the eggs" in order to organize and implement the aspect of his teaching that was spiritual activism. They are especially involved in Amnesty International.

Pir Vilayat stressed the idea of living a deeply spiritual life in the midst of the world. He spoke of Christ often. These are some of his words: "The belief in Christ is in the church, the book of Christ is with the clergy, the spirit of Christ is in the illuminated soul. The spirit of Christ can be traced in his own words where he said, 'I am the Alpha and Omega, I am the first and the last.' By this he meant, 'I was before Jesus was born, and I shall be after Jesus has gone.'" The Course refers to this spirit of Christ as the *Holy Spirit.*

Pir Zia Inayat Khan speaks of the first contact the Sufis had with Christianity. "Alienated by the betrayal of the spiritual integrity of Islam by venal empire-builders, the early Sufis struck out into the desert. Here they encountered Christian monastics whose humility and poverty deeply inspired them. The being of Jesus Christ seemed to resonate profoundly with the words of the Prophet Muhammad, 'My poverty is my pride.' On the example of the monastics, the early Sufis donned woolen robes. The word for wool in Arabic is *suf,* and some hold that this is the origin of the word *Sufi.*"

Sufism is akin to the Course in that it strips dogma from the Islamic religion just as the Course strips it from Christianity. The Course is Christianity par excellence and yet distinctly apart from the conventional understanding. Sufism is Islam par excellence and yet distinctly apart from it. Both insist on the reality behind ritual and symbol and both encourage a universal experience of God.

Both Sufism and the Course provide a program of spiritual training to bring about deep personal transformation, culminating in a balanced, harmonious and creative life. Both are inclusive and promote understanding and acceptance among adherents of various faiths so that the bias of faiths and beliefs may fall away. Both lead adherents toward a common spiritual experience. Both take away the boundaries that divide us by bringing into full light the underlying wisdom in which we are united.

A description of Sufism that rings true for me is, "It is the vocation and the discipline and the science of plunging into revelation and being drawn back with it to its Eternal Source." We could say the same of the Course. Because neither of these paths demands dogma, we are gently led to discover the truth resonating in our own hearts. Another description of the Sufi is a "Son or Daughter of the Moment." The Course asks us to see this life as a dream and to practice living in the present or "holy instant."

Many people who would like to be committed to the practice of either Sufism or the Course are unwilling do so because to commit to either calls for intensive discipline and would wreck their established patterns of thought. Both Sufism and the Course teach principles that fundamentalists view as radical. Although these teachings do not come under the term *religion* they are compatible with the writings of saints and mystics. To the Sufi, "The true religion is the sea of truth, and all the different faiths are its waves." Another way they view religion is that "All faiths are notes in the harmony of God."

Letting go of judgment is an often-recurring theme in both the Course and Sufism. The purpose of the Workbook is to train the mind in a systematic way to a different perception of everyone and everything in the world. It asks us not to judge the exercises but just to be willing to do them. Lesson 311 states:

> *Judgment was made to be a weapon used against the truth. It separates what it is being used against, and sets it off as if it were a thing apart. And then it makes of it what you would have it be. It judges what it cannot understand, because it cannot see totality and therefore judges falsely.*
>
> **W-P.II.311.1:1-4**

Pir Zia Inayat Khan, son of Pir Vilayat and now head of the Sufi Order of the West, relates a story of how his grandfather, Hazrat Inayat Khan, approached prejudice from a member of the audience he was addressing. "How could you *dare* mention the name of Muhammad in the same breath as our Lord Jesus Christ? Are you trying to tell me that they are equals?" His calm reply was disarming. "Madam, I did not say they are equals, but simply that I do not consider myself equal to the task of judging between them."

I personally see both Sufism and the Course as prime examples of sacred psychology, which is becoming more acceptable today. The proliferation of books containing interpretations of Rumi's poems has introduced Sufism into common Western culture. The precepts of the Course are becoming more accepted and one can find quotes from both Sufism and the Course in many books and magazines. In fact, when one becomes aware of them, they seem to be everywhere.

Sufism is often taught by direct methods such as gesture, symbol, and demonstration, which lead to many conflicting interpretations. This disagreement also exists within the Course community. Mysticism can never be static or stale. Sometimes authors have watered down both teachings to appeal to those not willing to do the actual work of transformation. Books about the Course or Sufism may give one the *conviction* of the mind but *certainty* only comes from direct experience and is sometimes known as "heart wisdom."

Sufis state that there is a form of knowledge that can be attained by man, which is of such an order that it is to scholastic learning as adulthood is to infancy. This is attained through practices and meditation. The Course satisfies our thirst for scholastic understanding with the Text and the Teacher's Manual. Direct practice is offered through the Workbook. The goal of both cultures is the surrender of self to the Self, which leads to unity and the experience of oneness with the Creator.

Sufis contend that a great part of Sufism must be personally communicated between a student and teacher. The teacher is often called "Murshid." The only teacher the Course recommends is its author, Jesus, whom we are asked to view as both teacher and elder brother. Jesus and the Holy Spirit are seen as the same teacher. Both paths set forth the premise that we are not actually taught but that the teacher awakens us to what we already know. Both agree that the spiritual path is an inward path that one treads toward the innermost Self, where one finds the life of God.

One aspect of the Course that is very different from Sufism is the use of male pronouns, "Father," "Sonship," etc. Sufis refer to God as "the One," "Friend," or "the Beloved," which is more in keeping with both masculine and feminine spirituality. When I created my first business cards I named my work, "My Father's Business." I soon changed that as it proved to be a separating title. I have met many women who refused to study the Course because they no longer wanted to relate to an all-male God.

Sufism cannot be reduced to the Qur'an or the Islamic religion any more than the Course can be reduced to three books or contemporary Christianity. Both Sufism and the Course call one to a way of life. Neither belongs to any country. There are Hindu Sufis, Muslim Sufis, Jewish Sufis and Christian Sufis. People of all religions have studied the Course and followed its disciplines. Both Sufism and the Course call for a life of discipline, for only prayer, meditation, and contemplation can open the door to true vision. Strict adherence to the suggested disciplines leads one to a kind of mysticism that is difficult to define.

A popular Sufi quote is, "The bee gathers honey from many flowers." Whereas Sufis study all sacred scripture and say that Jesus is God's "Miracle" and that Muhammad is God's "Messenger," the Course reinterprets the concepts of conventional Christianity.

Dhu al-Nun, a great early Sufi saint, defined the "perfect person" as "One who is as he was, before he was as he was." In both Sufism and the Course, we are called to sacrifice every belief that does not foster love. The Course tells us that we are love itself: *"Teach only love for that is what you are"* (T-6.I.13:2). Sufism sees the world as a series of veils that hide the Beloved. The Course agrees that the world we see is a projection of the mind that obscures true Reality.

Both Sufism and The Course call for total surrender to the Creator, the Beloved. Both call one to go within and listen for the voice for God. It is difficult to describe either one in any depth because so much of both disciplines consist of direct experience. What Christianity has called "sin," the Course sees as a less-helpful choice and encourages us to "choose again." The Sufis prefer to call these less-helpful choices "distractions."

The Course instructs us to study the Text and do the exercises set forth in the Workbook. The Sufis use meditation, music, dance, story telling, chanting, drumming, and humor for the inward transformation of the imagination or the subconscious. Both paths seek to change the mind. Both are pathways from natural hypocrisy to spiritual sincerity.

In 1977, I didn't know anyone else interested in the Sufis or studying the Course. It was a lonely journey for me until I started a group to share the Course. Gradually, I introduced the Course to many people and it became my main source of inspiration and study. There are no Sufis in my area but I drum and read Sufi literature and poetry along with my continued study of the Course, and am constantly thrilled with my experience of how they fit together as clasped hands. I believe both offer perennial wisdom at its best.

Before any garden or grape or wine existed
Our soul was drunk on eternal wine.
In the Baghdad of Eternity, we all proclaimed ecstatically:
"I am the Supreme Reality!"

RUMI

Clarice O'Bryan, a student and teacher of the Course since 1977, is a Transformation Artist who incorporates mentoring, guided imagery and bodywork, including labyrinth walks, into her private practice. She lives near Owensboro, KY., with her husband, Ron Mayhew. They have five children, fourteen grandchildren and ten great-grandchildren.
clarcoach@aol.com.

Chapter 12

Quakers

Jean Garman

I have always considered Quakers as progressive. From the beginning, founder, George Fox, did away with rituals and intermediaries, saying that people did not need anything between themselves and God. He seemed to understand that the more complex our hierarchies become, the more illusions are placed between ourselves and our experience of God. This is just one idea that struck me as a similarity between Quaker philosophy and *A Course in Miracles.* Truth is Truth, but certain aspects of Truth are often expressed more clearly in one spiritual discipline than in another. However, George Fox's visions coincide remarkably well with the writings of Helen Schucman of the Course. I am so grateful for having learned both of these loving disciplines. Quakers have taught me to see *That of God in everyone* and that naturally segues into seeing *That of God* in other faiths and all things.

George Fox believed in continuing revelation, and for this reason we should celebrate any readings or ideology that bring us to a higher way of seeing or experiencing our divine nature. Many have been raised with an idea that we should *stick with our own.* But hasn't this only reinforced our feelings of separation, superiority, defensiveness, and polarity? It is important to have spiritual writings and new references to help us *grow in the light.* It's limiting to only recognize God within our own camp and it serves to keep us separate. As we grow in this global community, we need to embrace Truth from many disciplines in order to appreciate people from other faiths and cultures. God is truly not only a God for Christians any more than He is only a God for Americans. As the Course puts it, we need to let go of the idea of *scarcity* and start living in *abundance.* This is a way of being that sees and celebrates God in all (people, philosophies, ideas), realizing it does not limit, but only adds.

Both the Course and Quakers recognize Jesus as our guide, believe in direct communion with Holy Spirit (or our Higher Selves), and reject doctrines or creeds set up by the Christian church. George Fox taught that God was in everyone, so "George Fox began preaching that since there was 'that of God in every man,' a formal church structure and educated ministry were unnecessary" (http://mb-soft.com/believe/txc/quakers.htm).

The Course teaches that hierarchy of any kind tends to take us from spirit and makes us see from our ego or human/carnal way. So, although it is necessary to have structure, both paths caution about the difficulty of staying with the Divine while trying to make structure. This is an important thing to keep at the forefront of our thoughts, because it is so easy to fool ourselves we are doing something good that, when really examined, leads away from spirit rather than towards it. The Quaker idea of *discernment* suggests carefully checking to see that we are coming from a place of spirit over human understanding. Spirit is always concerned in the best interest of all, since we truly are all One. The study of the Course clearly brings this out, and Quakers have always cared to work for the highest good of all.

George Fox and the Inner Journey

George Fox was a searcher. He found God by going within. The following two passages show the inner journey that is so necessary to finding the Peace of God.

"One morning... a great cloud came over me... and (then) a true voice arose in me, which said, "There is a living God who made all things."...Immediately the cloud and temptation vanished away, and life rose over it all; my heart was glad, and I praised the living God.

"...wonderful depths were opened unto me, beyond what can by words be declared; and (I came) to know the hidden unity in the Eternal Being" (*The First Years of Ministry, 1648-1649*, Chapter II).

The Course describes this inner journey and gives us a road map to this place within by doing the 365 Workbook lessons. Throughout the Course, it speaks of *clouds* and *veils* that hide the Truth of God, as George Fox mentions in the first paragraph above. The last phrase, "the hidden unity in the Eternal Being," speaks to metaphysical aspects of oneness and time vs. eternity. The Course teaches there is no death and that we truly are eternal spirit and can experience this right here and now. In fact, what keeps us from remembering this at any time is simply the clouds of ego thoughts and conditioning.

Questioning orthodox teachings during Fox's day was forbidden by law. Fox once landed in prison for confronting a preacher for placing scripture above the Voice for God. He stated that it is not the scriptures but what the scriptures point to—the Holy Spirit, which is available to us all!—that is important. Fox noted that Jews missed the message of Jesus because they relied on what they had made sacred—their scriptures—and so missed the gift they would have received if they used their inner knowing—their connection with Holy Spirit. When we get too dogmatic about things, including our religion or spirituality, we lose our spirit, for we are then investing in concrete form and forgetting about the ephemeral spirit of love and forgiveness. This is not to say either should be denied, but when we give emphasis to one over the other, we get out of balance. The Course points this out in various ways, reminding us that it is our choice in each moment whether we will invest in our human understanding (ego) or spirit, which is a higher authority (God and love).

George Fox describes his mission as follows: "I was sent to...(direct) them to the Spirit and grace of God in themselves, and to the Light of Jesus in their own hearts; that they might come to know Christ, their free teacher, to bring them salvation, and to open the Scriptures to them" *(One Man May Shake the Country for Ten Miles—1651-1652,* Ch. V*)*.

This speaks of our inner journey. It's interesting that Fox directs them to "the Light of Jesus... so that they might come to know Christ," because it sounds as if he is saying that Jesus is different than Christ. This correlates well with the Course, which explains that Christ is not only Jesus, but we are all part of Christ. George Fox seems to be saying that once we reach this understanding, the Scriptures can be opened to us because now we understand they can help us awaken to our true *Christ-conscious* selves.

Christ Consciousness or the Oneness of Us All

The Course teaches that we are all One. This Oneness is Christ. Jesus is as an elder brother to us because he *lived* this belief fully, thus, showing us the way to live as he lived, in Christ. George Fox states: "But I showed that the promises were to the Seed, not to many seeds, but to one Seed, Christ; who was one in male and female; for all were to be born again before they could enter into the kingdom of God" *(A Visit to Oliver Cromwell—1653-1654*, Ch. III).

Again, this confirms the understanding George Fox had of us all being part of this Oneness of Christ (Seed, not seeds) and that we would have to be "born again" (or re-perceive this understanding) in order to enter into the kingdom of God (Heaven).

Sin

At Derby, England, George Fox was taken away and questioned by authorities for his heretical preaching. After many hours of questioning, "At last they asked me whether I was sanctified. I answered, 'Yes; for I am in the paradise of God.' Then they asked me if I had no sin. I answered, 'Christ my Saviour has taken away my sin; and in Him there is no sin.' They asked how we knew that Christ did abide in us. I said, 'By His Spirit, that He hath given us.' They temptingly asked if any of us were Christ. I answered, 'Nay; we are nothing; Christ is all.' They said, 'If a man steal, is it no sin?' I answered, 'All unrighteousness is sin'" (*A Year In Derby Prison, 1650-1651*, Ch. IV, para. 10).

The Course says there is no *sin* (as popularly defined) but only *error*, which is choosing to believe we are *separate from God.* Fox *seems* inconsistent in his quote for he says, "Christ... has taken away my Sin; and in Him there is no sin." but later states, "All unrighteousness is sin." The Course helps clarify what this means by explaining that while we are in the world, which it calls *illusion* since it is not what we truly are (spirit), we can choose through our *wrong mind* which is aligned with ego, over our *right mind* which is aligned with spirit. All unrighteousness would simply be choosing with our wrong mind. Thus, we would be choosing from a position of being *separate from God* or from a position of sin or error.

Metaphysics and the Illusion

The following was written in a letter to Quaker Friends from Fox: "All along ye may see, by faith the mountains were subdued...Though the waves and storms be high, yet your faith will keep you…and the Truth is without time. Therefore keep on the mountain of holiness, ye who are led to it by the Light.

"Do not think that anything will outlast the Truth…For the good will overcome the evil; the light, darkness; the life, death; virtue, vice; and righteousness, unrighteousness. The false prophet cannot overcome the true; but the true prophet, Christ, will overcome all the false" (*At the Work of Organizing, 1667-1670*, Ch. XVII).

Here Fox speaks of time vs. eternity. He exhorts us to "keep on the mountain of holiness" or to stay in our right mind connected with Holy Spirit, so that we stay true to our eternal selves and are not tempted by the temporal. The false prophet is what the Course calls ego. Like the Course, he focuses Quaker Friends on the Truth of their eternal spirit, rather than investing in what they see in this world of time and ego illusion.

Regarding his vision of the New Jerusalem he wrote: "…I saw the beauty and glory of it, the length, the breadth, and the height thereof, all in complete proportion. I saw that all who are within the Light of Christ, and in His faith, of which He is the author; and in the Spirit, the Holy Ghost, which Christ and the holy prophets and apostles were in; and within the grace, and truth, and power of God, which are the walls of the city;—I saw that such are within the city, are members of it, and have right to eat of the Tree of Life..."

Here he is stating that these members are not only within the city but are the spirit, faith, and walls. Thus, they must be "one" with the city—they are part of this New Jerusalem or, as the Course calls it, "heaven" or "the real world." In the Course, when we reach the real world, it will be when we are living on Earth as One. We will know that we are truly dependent on one another, not in a co-dependent way but because we are truly One. Our minds, thoughts, and energy affect the consciousness of the planet, so we need to realize our interdependence and that we "go together or not at all" since we are all part of the one Son of God. According to the Course, until we all understand this and are united, we cannot return to heaven.

Social Activism

Most Quakers are social activists. Some Course students surmise that since the world is an illusion, there is no sense trying to *fix* it since *It* does not exist. However, Ken Wapnick, perhaps the foremost authority on the Course, who edited it with Helen and has written numerous books on it, states how difficult it is to be involved in political activism and remain spiritually-based rather than falling into ego dynamics. This is due to the fact that politics is largely an ego-based sphere. Ken said, however, "that if Course students really understood the Course, they would be able to do political activism in a most effective and uniting way."

They would be truly transformative activists because they would understand how important it is to stay in spirit and be ever watchful for ego tricks that can stumble and set us and our ideals back years. Thus, it seems it would be most expedient for Quakers and others sincere activists to do a deep study of the Course. On the more superficial layers, the Course may not sound applicable to social action, since it sees the world as illusion. However, when it is truly understood, it helps us to "be in the world but not of the world" so that we can remain in spirit while working in this ego-driven environment.

The Course suggests that there must be change, but sees it first and foremost as a change in our *minds*. Yet, as our minds are transformed, so are our actions and we affect the collective consciousness of all. Thus, the world can be transformed, one separated mind at a time and these transformed minds affect those around them. The above quotes from George Fox show that he also spoke of seeing the world through transformed eyes, after aligning ourselves with Holy Spirit.

Gathered Meetings

The Quaker "gathered meeting" can be compared with the Course concept of a "holy instant." Sometimes a Quaker meeting will be noticed to be a *gathered meeting*. This means that those who are sitting in the meeting have a feeling of *oneness*. It is as if all tensions and thoughts have dissolved and there is a feeling of unity or joy in the air. Likewise, in one experience of the holy instant there can be a similar feeling between two or more individuals when differences fall away and they experience a common purpose, usually closely tied to love and forgiveness.

This comparison has helped me bridge my perceived gap between Quaker philosophy and the Course. I hope it will also help others understand the need to study many inspired writings, to become stronger in understanding the divine that dwells within, and let this reign supreme over any church, doctrine, or attitude.

Jean Garman has always been puzzled about why humans try to improve the world while simultaneously engaging in endless bickering. She sought answers through numerous paths, culminating in *A Course in Miracles*. She received her Ordained Ministerial Counselor certificate from Pathways of Light, and spent several years studying with Dr. Kenneth Wapnick and his staff at the Foundation for *A Course in Miracles*. Jean holds an MS in Teaching from SUNY in New Paltz, NY, and tutors children. She has two grown daughters and currently lives in Riverside, CA with her partner, Dr. Dennis Jackson. weston.jean@gmail.com

Section III

New Thought

Chapter 13

Christian Science

Lynne R. Matous

Sunday School: A Lifelong Blessing

Prior to helping Helen Schucman scribe *A Course in Miracles* (from 1965 to 1972), William Thetford had a spiritual background that included Christian Science. Before reading the Course for the first time in 1992, I also had received teachings in Christian Science as a child and teenager while attending Christian Science Sunday Schools. What I'd learned about spiritual truth from Sunday school was alive and real for me and laid the foundation for my understanding and appreciating the value of *A Course in Miracles* when I read the text.

In the mid 1920s, when my father, George S. Rickenbach, was a young man, he chanced to attend a lecture on Christian Science in his hometown of Pittsburg, Pennsylvania. He was so impressed by the message of truth in this lecture that he became a church member. Not long after, he married, and with the demands of work and eventually a family (I was the youngest of four daughters), he no longer attended church. However, the teachings of Christian Science remained close to his heart and mind for all of his life.

While I was a child growing up in Cleveland, Ohio, in the 1940s, our family attended Christian Science services. These were memorable times for me because I would attend Sunday School, where I heard for the first time that I was God's perfect child—as was everyone—and nothing could alter this eternal Truth. So deep and beautiful was the truth I learned that I, like my father, held it close to my mind and heart, and it ever-after influenced my view of who and what I am, and everyone is.

One day, while playing with another little girl in our neighborhood, I realized the value of the truths I'd learned in Sunday school. Suddenly, in the midst of our play, the little girl stopped, and with a distressed look on her face, said: "Aren't you afraid of going to hell?" Knowing from Sunday school teachings that God is Love, I was shocked that she could even think such a thing, and I replied softly, "No. There is no such place as hell."

I had read and contemplated many times these words on the wall of the Christian Science Sunday school meeting room: "God is Love" (I John 4:8) and "Ye shall know the truth, and the truth shall make you free." (John 8:32) I still remember one of the first Sunday school classes I attended, where we discussed the synonyms for God. When it was my turn to name one, I said, "Goodness." I quickly and easily learned the seven synonyms for God in Christian Science: Life, Truth, Love, Spirit, Mind, Soul, and Principle. Later, I remember learning that we are made in the image and likeness of God—Spirit—and therefore are not the body—matter. Riding home in the car that Sunday, I looked down at my hand—realizing with some amazement that I was neither my hand nor the body attached to my hand.

After our family moved to Miami, Florida, in 1951, I started attending the Christian Science Sunday school in Coral Gables, where I learned many beautiful truths: Not only are we made in the image and likeness of God but also we are one with God—as the sun's rays are one with the sun.

During my teenage years (through the age of 18), I regularly attended Christian Science Sunday school and deeply appreciated the peace of mind resulting from the teachings. When I was 15 years old, I remember having a conversation about religion with a friend from high school. He emphatically said that there was no evidence for the existence of God. Without forethought, I blurted out: "*You* are the proof for the existence of God!" That ended the conversation.

Similar to the teachings of *A Course in Miracles*, our oneness with God was a fundamental teaching in Christian Science Sunday school. Also, similar to the Course, we were taught that Jesus is our way-shower—leading us back to the remembrance of this Truth. Additionally, the spiritual significances of Biblical passages were explained. For example, the freeing of the Israelites from slavery to Pharaoh symbolized our being freed from bondage to error, or mortal mind (the ego thought system in the Course). Similarly to the teaching of Jesus and the Holy Spirit in *A Course in Miracles*, we were taught that Jesus (our Way-shower) demonstrated the power and importance of knowing and choosing the Truth over error, or the lies of mortal mind (the ego in the Course).

As in the Course, the fundamental truth taught in Christian Science Sunday school is that everyone is God's perfect child (Spirit/Love, not matter/discord). Any seeming evidence to the contrary is error, or the thinking of mortal mind. Therefore, if we or someone we know displays disharmony, whether physical or mental, we are to "know the Truth" of their perfect oneness with God, and not support the illusion of mortal mind, therefore strengthening error. We were taught that to think or speak ill of anyone is "mental malpractice," while knowing the Truth of and for another (seemingly in need) not only helps him or her but strengthens our abidance in Truth. So, we were often reminded to "Stand porter at the door of thought" (*Science and Health with Keys to the Scriptures*, Mary Baker Eddy, pg. 392), admitting only thoughts of Truth.

Compatible with the essence of *A Course in Miracles*, the following passage ("the scientific statement of being") from *Science and Health* (pg. 468) is read at the close of all church and Sunday school services:

> *There is no life, truth, intelligence, nor substance in matter. All is infinite Mind and its infinite manifestation, for God is All-in-all. Spirit is immortal Truth; matter is mortal error. Spirit is the real and eternal; matter is the unreal and temporal. Spirit is God, and man is His image and likeness. Therefore man is not material; he is spiritual.*

The essential meaning of the above passage is captured in the following shorter quote from *A Course in Miracles*:

At no single instant does the body exist at all.

T-18.VII.3:1

Lynne R. Matous, MA has a master's degree in English literature and undergraduate degrees in both English and philosophy. She has taught writing at the University of Miami and Palm Beach Community College. An ordained interfaith minister, she is a graduate of All Faiths Seminary International's Class of 2010. She resides in Jupiter, Florida, where she enjoys editing books and articles and occasionally writing poetry. lmatous@yahoo.com

Chapter 14

Christian Science

Lorri Coburn

The Course and Christian Science are categorized as metaphysical teachings stemming from New Age or New Thought principles. While there is a great deal of overlap, both expand upon New Thought ideas. The Course and Christian Science are among the few thought systems that not only teach non-duality—that only God and His ideas exist—but insist on it in practice. Most metaphysical philosophies meld matter and spirit, while the Course and Christian Science adhere to a firm distinction between the two.

Controversy

Christian Science has been surrounded by controversy since Mary Baker Eddy discovered it in 1866. After a severe fall on ice in which she was not expected to live, Eddy had an epiphany about the nature of God. She realized that God was not *in* a material universe, but in a spiritual universe. God is not *in* the apparent physical world, because all matter is an illusion. God, being only Love, cannot contain both good and evil. Therefore, evil—sin, death, illness, lack, etc.—does not, and *has never* existed. This revelation healed her, and Eddy spent the next 45 years expanding her understanding of the nature of God.

In an age when women had no voting rights and could not own property, Eddy established the First Church of Christ, Scientist, the Pulitzer Prize-winning newspaper the *Christian Science Monitor*, and a publishing company for her books, including the primary text for Christian Scientists, *Science and Health with Key to the Scriptures (S & H)*. Their other main text is the *inspired* word of the Bible, which is a metaphysical interpretation. In church services, the *pastor* is the Bible and *Science and Health*, and sermons are readings selected from these books. This avoids ego specialness, even though they don't use that familiar term from the Course.

Christian Science is often labeled a *cult* by fundamental Christians, and this charge has also been leveled at the students of *A Course in Miracles.* Any teaching that reinterprets or expands upon mainstream doctrine can be perceived as threatening. The unwavering stance that God is not in matter (Course term: *form*) is the source of many of the controversies around Christian Science. Further, both teachings state that Jesus was a man who recognized his oneness with God, thus, embodying the Christ. This diverges from orthodox Christian doctrine that Jesus was divine, sent by God as a sacrifice for man's sin. Jesus states in the Course that he did not suffer on the cross, while Christian Scientists tend to believe that he suffered because his resurrection and ascension were not quite complete. Neither Christian Science nor the Course adheres to the idea that man is sinful, and, further, both state that sin is unreal.

The World

Christian Scientists frequently cite the *first* Biblical account of creation, in which "God pronounced good all that He created, and the Scriptures declare that he created all" (*S & H*, p. 526). They distinguish this from the *second* account of creation, which describes man's fall from grace in the Garden of Eden. They make the point that only the first account is true. "The 'tree of life' stands for the erroneous doctrine that the knowledge of evil is as real, hence as God-bestowed, as the knowledge of good" (*S & H*, p. 526). Both the Course and Christian Science declare that evil is unreal and that the separation from God never happened.

At first glance it looks like Christian Science differs from the Course, because the Course states, *"The world you see is an illusion of a world. God did not create it, for what He creates must be eternal as Himself"* (C-4.1:1-2). But it's the *material* world to which both teachings refer. "Spirit never created matter" (*S & H*, p. 335). Form/matter must decay and die by its very nature. Since death is not an attribute of God, God cannot create matter. Both systems indicate that the *real world* of God is formless Mind, containing only Love and Life. God is not *in* the physical world; however, the physical world *can reflect* God. Beautiful things reflect *ideas.* "...human belief misinterprets nature. Arctic regions, sunny tropics, giant hills, winged winds, mighty billows, verdant vales, festive flowers and glorious heavens,—all point to Mind, the spiritual intelligence they reflect" (*S & H*, p. 240).

> *In you is all of Heaven. Every leaf that falls is given life in you. Each bird that ever sang will sing again in you. And every flower that ever bloomed has saved its perfume and its loveliness for you. What aim can supersede the Will of God and of His Son, that Heaven be restored to him for whom it was created as his only home? Nothing before and nothing after it. No other place; no other state nor time. Nothing beyond nor nearer. Nothing else. In any form. This can you bring to all the world...*
>
> **T-25.IV.5:1-11**

Physical Healing

Some people feel that Eddy stole her ideas from Phineas Quimby, considered by many to be the father of New Thought. Eddy studied under Quimby and was healed of several illnesses with his help. However, when she fell on the ice, her understanding took the next step to non-duality. (Her fall happened *after* Quimby's death.) Eddy realized that *all is mind*, not that both matter *and* mind exist. She explains in her writings that Quimby used the mind to heal the body, while making the body/matter *real*. Eddy experienced the *total non-reality* of the physical world, in which *there can be no illness*. This is a f*undamentally different framework* than the idea that matter can be infused with and healed by Spirit. "Spirit, Soul, is not confined in man, and is never in matter" (*S & H*, p. 467).

> *You see the flesh or recognize the spirit. There is no compromise between the two. If one is real the other must be false... At no single instant does the body exist at all.*
>
> **T-31.VI.1:2-3; T-18.VII.3:1**

Another controversial aspect of Christian Science is its stance on medicine. Both the Course and Christian Science scoff at the idea that drugs, supplements, proper hygiene, etc., are what keep the body healthy. "How do drugs...heal? It may be affirmed that they do not heal, but only relieve suffering temporarily, exchanging one disease for another" (*S & H*, p. 483).

> *What the world perceives as therapeutic is but what will make the body "better." Its forms of healing thus must substitute illusion for illusion. One belief in sickness takes another form and so the patient now perceives himself as well. He is not healed. He merely had a dream that he was sick, and in the dream he found a magic formula to make him well. Yet he has not awakened from the dream. There is no remedy the world provides that can effect a change in anything. The mind that brings illusions to the truth is really changed. There is no change but this.*
>
> W.P.I.140.1:2,4,5; 2:1-3; 7:3-5

> *You really think a small round pellet or some fluid pushed into your veins through a sharpened needle will ward off disease and death.*
>
> W-P.I.76.3:3

Contrary to popular opinion, Christian Science does not *forbid* one to use drugs or go to doctors. However, it is strongly encouraged to rely only on God for healing because that is the way one gains the understanding that *only God's creation is real.* There is a strong emphasis on the *demonstration of physical healing,* but that is only to help us learn that the world and body are not real and we can truly depend on God for all things. Likewise, the Course tells us,

> *Miracles demonstrate that learning has occurred under the right guidance, for learning is invisible and what has been learned can be recognized only by its results.*
>
> T-12.VII.1:1

What heals the body in both systems is the understanding that the body *is not real.* "...the Christian Scientist takes the best care of his body when he leaves it most out of his thought, and like the Apostle Paul, is 'willing rather to be absent from the body, and to be present with the Lord'" (*S & H*, p. 383). Likewise, the Course tells us that to accomplish healing of any kind, not just bodily healing, "*the insignificance of the body must be an acceptable idea*" (M-5.II.3:12).

Eddy stressed that her discovery was *Science*, not faith, because it follows laws and is exacting and true in every instance. Eddy believed that her discovery was of the Truth principles that Jesus used to heal. "It is plain that God does not employ drugs or hygiene, nor provide them for human use; else Jesus would have recommended and employed them in his healing" (*S & H*, p. 143). Eddy avoided use of the word "miracle," because the healings she performed were not random acts of divine intervention, rather, based on *Principle*. Christian Science has healed consistently for over a hundred years. Thousands upon thousands of healings are recorded; testimonies are available online at www.jsh.christianscience.com.

Many people erroneously think that Christian Scientists employ "faith healing." This again implies that something "real,"—the body—is made well through faith. While the Course uses the term "miracle," its definition of a miracle is more in line with *Science* than with a supernatural act of beneficence.

> *Miracles are natural. When they do not occur something has gone wrong. A miracle is a correction. It does not create, nor really change at all. It merely looks on devastation, and reminds the mind that what it sees is false. It undoes error.*
>
> T-1.I.6:1-2; W-P.II.13.1:1-4

Daily Practice

A major difference between the Course and Christian Science is the Course's emphasis on ego dynamics. The Course spends a great deal of time explaining special relationships, the murderous thought system of the ego, the projection of guilt, and the belief in separation from God. We are taught that as we forgive our brothers, we awaken to our true Identity as the holy Son of God. Christian Science emphasizes being aware of ourselves as the expression and reflection of God's qualities, which includes forgiveness.

Eddy's term for *ego* is *mortal mind*. Rather than explaining *how* mortal mind works, Eddy simplifies it to a false belief in matter. "To mortal mind, matter is substantial, and evil is real. Disease is an experience of so-called mortal mind. In reality, there is no *mortal* mind…" (*S & H*, pp. 292, 493, 103).

In the Course, the only problem is a belief in separation and the main solution is forgiveness. This is alternately called *accepting Atonement*, awakening from the dream, choosing the Holy Spirit's thought system or accepting our true Identity. Christian Science recognizes the same basic error and solution, but simplifies it: deny the reality of mortal mind/ego, and in its place, accept oneself as created in the image and likeness of God. "Our law refuses to recognize Man as sick or dying, but holds him to be forever in the image and likeness of his Maker" (*S & H*, p. 441). The Course emphasizes the word *choice*, while Christian Scientists encourage *leaning on and yielding to God*.

To become aware of how we are made in God's image, Christian Science focuses on how we express God through His seven primary names or attributes: Mind, Principle, Love, Life, Soul, Spirit, and Truth. Christian Science stresses God's goodness, love, and care for us. Its main focus is to depend on God for *everything*, to *start with God* rather than starting with undoing ego guilt, and to listen to God's thoughts about how *God* sees us. Prayer is a process of *reasoning* that problems cannot be from God, and since we are created by God and He is constantly activated through us, we actually have no problems. This is similar to the Course's emphasis on reason and recognizing that we have no problems because the separation never happened.

The Course trains our minds to listen to the Holy Spirit so we can receive God's love, especially in the second half of the Workbook. "*I am as God created me*" (W-p.I.94.h) is repeated 144 times in various forms (which seems to be Jesus' nod to numerology). This is the same as "I am created in the image and likeness of God" (Genesis 1:26).

Here are some actual, typical conversations that have occurred between my Christian Science practitioner and me that highlight the similarities and differences in terminology, emphasis and practice:

> Me: My anger and guilt have been kicking up lately, and I think that's because I'm getting closer to God and the ego is shrieking in fear.
>
> Practitioner: There is no part of you that is afraid. There is no part of you that is not already whole and part of God, because

God created you and you don't contain anything unlike God. You already love God completely.

Me: My illness is getting worse. I think that's because I still haven't forgiven this man who betrayed me. I also feel bad because I hurt him deeply and projected my guilt onto him. I know it's all a dream, but it doesn't feel like it.
Practitioner: *Start with God* instead of illusion. God judges you only as His image and likeness and that never contains illness. Error cannot cause illness; God is the only Cause. Illness is just an imposition, a false idea of mortal mind, and you don't have to believe that voice. You are both children of God and neither of you can be a victim nor victimizer. You're right—it was all a dream. The conflict *never happened*.

Me: I don't feel close to God. I got sick again because I felt guilty. I'm trying so hard to choose love over fear, but I still believe in the illusion. I'm not even sure I should expect healing of the body, because it's not real.
Practitioner: You *already* have an intimate connection with God because you are God's daughter. There is *no justification* for illness, so feeling guilty can't make you sick. The human mind says we have to work hard to forgive or align ourselves with God, but healing is about what *God* is doing *for* you. It's never about human will. In the Bible, Jesus never said, "The body isn't real, so just put up with it."

In summary, while there may be differences in terminology, daily practices, and emphases, there is basically no difference in the message of the Course and Christian Science. Both are paths up the same mountain to God's pinnacle.

Lorri Coburn, MSW, is the author of *Breaking Free: How Forgiveness and A Course in Miracles Can Set You Free*. Lorri has been a psychotherapist for 35 years, specializing in addictions, mood disorders, relationships and spirituality. Visit her website, www.lorricoburn.com to preview her book, ask questions about ACIM, and view YouTube videos.

Chapter 15

Unity

Doran Dibble

Years ago, I spent five weeks of study at Unity Village in preparation for their seminary. While I was there, I talked to lots of people—faculty and students—about the Course. Many had touched it in one way or another and saw mostly wonderful similarities, but some did not. In fact, Unity headquarters went through a period of shunning the Course. But, as I understand it, since "Unitics" and ministers across the country continued to be drawn to it, headquarters took another look and formally acknowledged the Course as a spiritual teaching, emphasizing that is not the same as Unity.

My intent in this article is to present some central Unity principles and Course principles, conveying the graceful alignment and interconnectedness I find there. Although I come across a wide range of *interpretations* of the principles of the Course and Unity, I feel the *principles* themselves are similar enough that comparing them is like comparing hot fudge sundaes from two ice cream stands. The basic ingredients have a lot in common. The dishes may have different shapes and the fudges different consistency, but what you experience within when you whole-heartedly devour either sundae minimizes the differences.

First Unity Principle

Unity's teachings are often summarized by the five basic Unity principles. Principle One is about what God is. It attests to the infiniteness and goodness of God: "God, Divine Mind, is the Source and Creator of all...The nature of God is absolute good" (*Twenty Questions and Answers about Unity.*). Put another way, "God is absolute good, everywhere present." (Taken from a Unity center's Sunday order of service.)

Course principles express that everything that really exists—all that is eternal, limitless, and unconditionally loving—is an extension of

God's love. Further, the Course states that what is not wholly loving—guilt, fear, separation, attack, and defense—does not really exist, except as illusion in our mind, and so is not of God. Therefore, God is not the Creator of guilt, fear, separation, attack, defense, and such. No matter how hard we may try to combine them, a fundamental tenet of the Course is that *"truth and illusions are irreconcilable"* (T-10.IV.2:5).

I will leave it at that, since any description of God is inherently flawed by the limitations of words and worldly concepts.

Second Unity Principle

Principle Two is about what We are—divine. This principle encompasses the Unity concepts of what we currently experience (called "manifest man") and what can be ("ideal man"). "We are spiritual beings, ideas in the Mind of God, created in His image and after His likeness. Ideal man is the perfect man, the Christ, the pattern every person is seeking to bring forth. Manifest man is the idea of perfection brought into expression according to the degree of understanding in the individual consciousness" (*Twenty Questions and Answers about Unity*).

The Course proclaims:

> *Christ is God's Son as He created Him. He is the Self we share, uniting us with one another, and with God as well. He is the Thought which still abides within the Mind that is His Source. He has not left His holy home, nor lost the innocence in which He was created. He abides unchanged forever in the Mind of God.*
>
> W-p.II.6.1:1-5

Our holiness—the Christ within—is not the result of anything we have accomplished or brought about. Rather, it is the result of God. (God took care of it in that whole Creation thing, and I don't know about you, but that gets a big "Amen!" from me.) When I remember that God is divine Cause and I am divine Effect, and that all the goodness I have and do comes from God, all is well. When I forget, all is hell!

This identity principle can be a real point of contention. Some folks feel that the Course has an unrealistic or harsh message that our true identity is Christ and that bodies are limited and separate and, therefore, illusory—not of God.

> *You see the flesh or recognize the spirit. There is no compromise between the two. If one is real the other must be false, for what is real denies its opposite.*
> **T-31.VI.1:1-3**

> *I am not a body. I am free.*
> *For I am still as God created me.*
> **W-p.I.201.h**

Some folks feel that Unity has a confusing message that our identity is both fully formless spirit and fully human form—which cannot coexist. I have heard that confusing message taught in Unity gatherings. I have also heard it taught in Course gatherings. To me, the message is a departure from foundational Unity teachings such as these by Charles Fillmore in *Talks on Truth*: "No one has even seen his real body as it is in the sight of God, except through the mind. The body of flesh, bones, and blood that the eye of sense beholds is not the true body any more than the heart of flesh is the true organ of love. 'That which is born of the flesh is flesh; and that which is born of the Spirit is spirit.' The 'flesh' is a state of consciousness; the 'Spirit' is a state of consciousness."

Third Unity Principle

The Third Principle is often called "the law of mind action: thoughts held in mind produce after their kind." This principle centers on thoughts as creative and powerful energies that bring forth everything. As Emilie Cady put it in *Lessons in Truth*, "The appearances are that our bodies and our circumstances control our thoughts, but the opposite is true. Our thoughts control our bodies and our circumstances."

The Course's teaching is quite similar: *"All thinking produces form at some level,"* and *"As a man thinketh, so does he perceive"* (T-2.VI.9:14; T-21.In.1:6). Thought is cause; perception and experience are the effects. What an empowering reversal of a commonly held belief about our relationship with the world. Your thoughts about your life and the world produce your experience of them, not the other way around. As explained in the Course: *"Perception is a mirror, not a fact. And what I look on is my state of mind, reflected outward"* (W-p.II.304.1:3-4). If I'm in an off mood, my experiences will be tainted. Conversely, when my thoughts are peaceful and joyous, everything follows suit.

Unity and the Course both present denials and affirmations as powerful tools for changing error thinking. In *Lessons in Truth*, Emilie Cady describes denial and affirmation as offering "what Jesus meant when He said, 'Whatever you ask for in prayer, believe that you have received it and it will be yours.'" The Course describes how miracles heal: *"because they deny body-identification and affirm spirit-identification"* (T-1.I.29:3).

There's no trick to denials and affirmations, no magic, though I often observe a significant imposition of magic in how they are interpreted, taught, and practiced. Denials and affirmations used for hiding from what's happening or pretending you are happy when you are not teach that your power lies in deception and dishonesty. But dishonesty does not lead to truth. Your real power lies in truth because it is of God. Proper use of denials and affirmations make you available for truth and genuine fulfillment by making room in your mind for what is beyond appearances. The Course describes the proper use of denial as denying *"the ability of anything not of God to affect you. It is not used to hide anything, but to correct error"* (T-2.II.1:11, 13).

What goes on in the mind is really something, isn't it? Thoughts are so powerful they give rise to whole worlds, as explained in the Course. The mind is like an experience generator. Whatever input you give it, an experience is generated in kind. Fear in, fear out; love in, love out. When we are willing to change our minds and let our attention be captivated only by loving thoughts, we get a glimpse of Heaven. But we can resist. Oh, can we resist! As Charles Fillmore explained in *Talks on Truth,* "Hence the cry goes up from all over the land, 'Heal me! Heal me!' as Jesus of Nazareth healed those who came to him, 'but don't ask me to change my ideas.'"

Fourth Unity Principle

Prayer is the subject of Unity's Fourth Principle. I realize that some consider meditation and prayer to be the same; others consider them to be different. To me, what matters is not what you call it but what you look to it for and receive from it. Prayer is such a personal and intimate aspect of one's spiritual path—how about we just love it without being distracted by labels?

Twenty Questions and Answers about Unity states that, to Jesus, prayer was "conscious communion with God." The authors of the Unity book, *The Simple Truth,* feel that "prayer is any conscious attempt to experience more of the presence of God." As the Course puts it: *"Prayer is the greatest gift with which God blessed His Son at his creation"* (S-1.in.1:1), and *"Prayer is the medium of miracles"* (T-1.I.11:1). (So I guess it is safe to assume that we're talking about a little more than getting a premonition about a winning lottery number.)

Regardless how commonplace it may be to see prayer as a means of getting worldly things, The Course and Unity principles teach that prayer progresses toward a higher purpose. The Course teaches that *"(prayer) does change in form, and grow with learning until it reaches its formless state, and fuses into total communication with God"* (S-1.II.1:3). *The Simple Truth* explains that "after prayer and meditation become an established habit with you, the two will begin to merge until eventually your quiet time is devoted solely to waiting in the Presence." Rev. Jim Rosemergy, Unity minister and former executive vice president of Unity School of Christianity, offers this: "Prayer's purpose is not to enlist Spirit's assistance in living a better human life ... but, instead, to awaken to our spiritual identity."

"Seek ye first the Kingdom of Heaven, and all these things shall be added unto you" (Matthew 6:33). This Bible passage is echoed by the Course and Unity. There can be a great temptation to seek first "all these things" and believe they will bring about the Kingdom. But worldly things are not the cause of the Kingdom, God is. The Course teaches, *"It is impossible to pray for idols and hope to reach God"* (S-1.I.1:5).

A moving example of seeking first the Kingdom is the covenant that Charles and Myrtle Fillmore entered into with Spirit: "We, Charles Fillmore and Myrtle Fillmore, husband and wife, hereby dedicate ourselves, our time, our money, all we have and all we expect to have, to the Spirit of Truth, and through it to the Society of Silent Unity. It being understood and agreed that said Spirit of Truth shall render unto us an equivalent for this dedication, in peace of mind, health of body, wisdom, understanding, love, life, and an abundant supply of all things necessary to meet every want without making any of these things the object of our existence."

Fifth Unity Principle

Walk the talk. Live your faith. That's what the Fifth Unity Principle is about. Unity World Headquarters' website puts it this way: "Knowledge of these spiritual principles is not enough. We must live them." We can do so by allowing the absolute Good in everything to be shown to us; embracing the Christ-consciousness in everyone; holding loving thoughts and releasing unloving ones; and praying to celebrate and deepen our awareness of God's Love. Although we may try to complicate the walk or hedge our faith with conditions and exceptions, the principles and our part in living them remain unchanged.

Just reading about or listening to your spiritual truth doesn't fulfill its goal any more than just ordering from a menu fills your belly. You need to dig in—taste it, savor it, and make it part of you. Buddha said, "However many holy words you read, however many you speak, what good will they do you if you do not act upon them?" It reminds me of a quote from Eric Butterworth. He noted that because there are so many wonderful books describing spiritual principles, it is easy to get "over-read and under-done."

The Course states, *"This is not a course in the play of ideas, but in their practical application"* (T-11.VIII.5:3). Nearly half of the Course is made up of 365 daily lessons (exercises) formed into a workbook. That is because *"it is doing the exercises that will make the goal of the Course possible"* (W-in.1:2). If you had a lamp with a magic genie inside and you wanted what it offered, wouldn't you rub the lamp? Well, the practical application of your spiritual truth offers far more than any genie fantasy. If it takes more than rubbing to bring it forth, so be it.

What about when things get bumpy? Myrtle Fillmore instructs us to let go of judgments that no longer serve our highest purpose. "You can bring these undesirable states to an end right now! First of all stop believing in them, and the necessity for them...Some new attitudes will be necessary. Some old customs and beliefs will have to be changed and given up." We may need help doing that when darkness obscures the light. Emmet Fox reminds us of the power of holding our gaze on the light: "Stop thinking about the difficulty, whatever it is, and think about God instead." The practice is to be faithful to a belief in God's eternal Presence in spite of any perceived darkness. Sure, there are times when you are certain your fearful thoughts and perceptions are real, but isn't there a chance you are wrong? As the Course puts it, *"Do you prefer that you be right or happy?"* (T-29.VII.1:9).

When can all of this really happen? Unity and the Course stress that the present moment is the time for experiencing God. *"The emphasis of this course always remains the same;—it is at this moment that complete salvation is offered you, and it is at this moment that you can accept it"* (M-24.6:1). The principles aren't just good-time principles any more than God is just a good-time God. To postpone living your spiritual principles in earnest until some time in the future when circumstances warrant it more is to misunderstand their power and delay the experience of God's glory, which is *Your* glory.

Doran Dibble often misperceives himself as an ACIM student, teacher and presenter, hi-tech professional, kidder, family man and dreamer who is guided by the Course's incredibly profound and practical message and Messenger. When Doran genuinely and wholeheartedly applies Course principles, miracles happen. Thank you, Jeeeesus! His first book isn't published yet, mainly because it isn't written yet. Doran welcomes comments and/or questions sent to dorandibble@gmail.com

Chapter 16

Science of Mind

R. Gordon Seeley

"Science of Mind" is the name Ernest Holmes (1887-1960) gave to his life's work. He was a student, mystic, teacher, and an integral part of America's New Thought spiritual movement that began in the mid-1800s. His early work was published as a small book in 1923, titled *Creative Mind.* Three years later, he released his major work titled *The Science of Mind.* He subsequently scripted hundreds of articles for sermons, magazines, and a syndicated radio program, many of which are available today as a book titled, *Living the Science of Mind.* (In 1927, Holmes and some of his followers began to meet formally and became known as The Church of Religious Science. To clarify, this paper is about Holmes' published work and is not intended to necessarily represent the teachings of the Church, or its affiliates.)

The subtitle of recent editions of *Science of Mind* reads: *A Philosophy, A Faith, A Way of Life.* In short, Science of Mind is not lightweight spirituality. Like the Course, it is vast in weight and depth. Yet, Holmes said the purpose of Science of Mind was simply: "...that the student may be able to apply his spiritual understanding to the everyday problems of human life." It turns out that Science of Mind is another wonderful example of what may be called "practical spirituality." Spirituality that really works! The difference between the Course and Science of Mind is mostly one of perspective, and I have divided this article into three parts: The first relates to their obvious differences, the second to their similarities, and the third to their oneness. In doing so, it should be said that, although I have been a student and a practitioner of the Course and Science of Mind for several years, my knowledge continues to be limited so I am presenting this article as a student, not as a teacher.

Differences

Looking with a critical eye, one can find many differences between the Course and Science of Mind, major and minor. For example, Science of Mind is far easier to read and comprehend than the Course. These days I read the Course with ease, but it took a long time before that happened. On the other hand, I never had a problem with Holmes. Not only does he write using contemporary language and style, but he is skilled at taking complex ideas and presenting them in a way that most people could understand. Science of Mind is also far easier on the mind from a psychological standpoint. The Course is an intentional mindbender, designed to erase ego and create a radically new worldview that is based on love. Letting go of our old ideas can be painful, and the Course inflicts great pain (imagined, of course) until a transition to right-mindedness is made.

Holmes gives a plausible, precise, almost scientific explanation of how thought takes form in the material world. (God's thought as well as our own.) He says that thought is a movement of Spirit acting upon Spiritual Substance; that God's Law receives these thoughts and transforms them into something more substantial, such as matter. He says God's Law is impartial, and that anyone (God or man) can use it and get the same results. He says that if we think like God we will get God-like results! Science of Mind teaches a form of panentheism, saying God is everything and everything is God. Everything we see is simply an extension of God, including ourselves. He refers to the universe, and everything in it, as "The Thought of God" and "The Body of God." Moreover, he doesn't believe that the natural world is an illusion: "Of all things on earth the human body is the most beautiful, the most wonderful and the most God-like.

When we behold a beautiful sunset we should see the wonderful thought of God, the radiance of his presence. In the strength of the hills we should see the strength of the Spirit; and seeing all things as spiritual ideas, we should learn to love them, because God has made them and given them to us to use. The soul who in ecstasy can rush up to a tree and embrace it realizes more of God than all the bigoted priests who have ever lived. The one who can sniff the ocean breeze with delight feels the presence of the divine being more keenly than does the one who kneels in despair before an awful God of Justice. Learn then how to appreciate Nature and Nature's God. Spend much time in the out of doors; look up at the stars; let them be your companions; tread the pathless ways of the trees and the giant forests and see God in everything that you look upon, the God of the everywhere" (*Creative Mind*).

Science of Mind's emphasis is on seeing perfection in everything, and especially in man. There is little talk of sin and hell. Sin is simply something that can be corrected with right thinking, and once we understand the problem, it says that we should withdraw our thoughts from the problem and place them on the solution. (The solution is seeing God's Perfection everywhere.) It can seem to newcomers that Science of Mind is materialistic, and, in a way, it is. Holmes was very concerned about our physical and material well-being, and made no apology for it. He said the Children of God have an absolute right to all the goodness God has to offer! Like Jesus, however, he also said that we must first seek the Kingdom of God, and then the rest will be added unto us in good measure.

Students of SOM are encouraged to perform spiritual healing work called "treatments." There's no direct physical contact, and it's really mental or thought healing because the healing takes place in the patient's mind. The idea is that healing the mind will heal the body. All SOM work actually takes place in God's Mind because, according to SOM, there is only One Mind. In other words, what we call "our mind" is simply part of God's Mind to be used as we see fit. We literally live and breathe and have our being within the confines of God's Mind, the implications of which are profound.

These are just a few of the differences that can be found between the Course and Science of Mind. At first, I thought some of them were important. As my study progressed, however, I began to see that they were more complementary than different.

Similarities

The function of the Course and Science of Mind is to help us change what we currently believe about life in order to improve our perception of life. The following quote reflects the similarity between Science of Mind and the Course: "To acquire the larger consciousness is no easy task. All that we have believed in which contradicts the perfect whole must be dropped from our thought, and we must come to realize that we are now living in a perfect universe, peopled with perfect spiritual beings, each of which (coupled with the Great Divinity) is complete within himself. We must see that we are one in the great one, and then we will not separate or divide, but unite and add, until in time we will find that we are living in an entirely different world from that in which we had once thought we were living" (*Creative Mind*). Holmes said that Science of Mind was simply a composite of the best ideas he found in world literature beginning with the Hindu Vedas on up to modern science. There is an emphasis on Man expressing himself as God in a world without limit.

Science of Mind theory rests strongly on God's Law regarding cause and effect. It is about how thoughts become conditions, and that if we want new conditions we must have new thoughts to bring them about. It is also about the Law of Correspondence, which states that there is a direct correlation between the kinds of thoughts we have and what they produce, and about the Law of Attraction, which brings things into our experience to match our thoughts (good or bad).

Oneness

The goal of most spiritual studies is for us to become mentally integrated with our Creator to the extent that "My thoughts are your thoughts." When man's thoughts are not God's thoughts, he suffers for it. Not at the hand of God, of course, but simply due to his own ignorance. The Course and SOM say that in order to be truly useful and happy a radical change must occur in our thinking. They help us change the contents of our mind through the use of powerful spiritual concepts, principles, and practices. They speak of attaining Christ Vision—literally seeing through the eyes of Christ. Both teach a strong case of non-duality in a form that literally says: "I and my Father are One!" Both have strong theoretical foundations. Both use impeccable logic throughout. Both reveal strong Christian and Eastern influences, but not their dogma. Both have strong connections to New Testament ideas and sayings that may make them seem somewhat Christian. With thoughts of separation gone, the only thing left is God and what He Created. We are left with wonderful spiritual things such as: love, joy, peace, patience, kindness, goodness, faithfulness, gentleness, and self-discipline (Galatians 5:22-23).

However, the most important thing we are left with when all our foolish thoughts are gone is our own True Self (the Son of God, Atman) and our beloved Creator, the Source of everything good in this, or any world.

Everyday Practice

Spiritual lessons are useless unless they are put into practice: "We are intelligent beings living in an intelligent universe that responds to our mental states, and insofar as we learn to control those mental states, we shall automatically control our environment. This is what is meant by the practical application of the principles of Science of Mind to the problems of everyday living. This is what is meant by demonstration." Holmes' Science of Mind demonstrations and treatments are similar to what the Course calls "miracles." The process is the same, and can be seen as one of spiritual forgiveness. We need not forgive people, places, or things, because they are not the cause of our troubles.

What we forgive, pardon, dismiss, let go and get rid of, are our old ideas—thoughts that seem to oppose God's Will. Knowing that all human problems trace back to our thinking, we replace wrong thinking with right thinking. We look past present appearances and allow the Power and Perfection of God to flow through us. The result is a grateful sense of Oneness in which freedom, happiness, peace, and prosperity come naturally and bountifully. We see the perfection of God in everyone and everything, knowing Joy of the Highest Order.

R. Gordon Seeley has been a Course student since 2005. He is retired and lives in Brick, NJ. He can be reached at: Oneness285@yahoo.com.

Chapter 17

Science of Mind

Rev. Ken Davis

There are many who mistakenly think that the teachings of Science of Mind (SOM) and *A Course in Miracles* are the same. Still others realize that there must be a difference, are not sure what it is, and are a little uncomfortable without knowing why. This discomfort becomes a small disturbance, like a minor troubling noise under the hood of a car. For Course students within the SOM community, the teachings of the Course could possibly become unclear.

My purpose is to:

1. Clarify this difference in the teachings, and in doing so,
2. Clarify a difficult teaching in the Course, and finally
3. Clarify the *meaninglessness* of this difference for students of the Course.

To begin with, there are remarkable similarities between the thought system of the Course and that of SOM. The most important commonality is the focus on the importance of our minds. This focus was considered revolutionary when the New Thought movement (re) introduced it!

The distinction between these two is very simple and it is a key factor for properly understanding both. The important difference between the metaphysics of the Course and SOM is simply this:

* SOM teaches that the world is real and is a manifestation of, and the Body of, God!
* The Course teaches that the world cannot be real and is made up by you, and not God, to justify the idea of separation from God.

OK! That's it. Thanks for your time! Have a great day! Thanks, again! Just kidding, everyone!

There are *many* direct and indirect references in the written record to show this point. Here are just two. From SOM:

WHAT IS THE BODY? Body is a concrete idea, existing in time and space, for the purpose of furnishing a vehicle through which Life may express Itself. The physical universe is the Body of God; it is a manifestation of the Mind of God, in form. It is that Creation which, while It may have beginnings and ends, of Itself neither begins nor ends. The Manifestation of Spirit is necessary if Spirit is to come into Self-Realization; hence, Body. The Science of Mind, Ernest S. Holmes

From the Course:

The world you see is an illusion of a world. God did not create it, for what He creates must be eternal as Himself. Yet there is nothing in the world you see that will endure forever.

C-4.1:1-3

This is not the only difference, but this is the *essential* difference and *most* of the other differences can be explained by this one. If you are participating in the SOM community and you are not clear about this difference, you might begin to think that the Course is saying something that it is not saying.

It is easy to fall into the conventional assumption that God made this world/universe. The idea that the world of form is an illusion is difficult to imagine. To struggle with this concept and integrate it into your thinking can be a steep hill fraught with fear.

Well, just *how* important is the mastery of this idea anyway? In other words, must a spiritual path or religion include this concept to be "true"? Per the Course, it is *not* important!

A universal theology is impossible, but a universal experience is not only possible but necessary.

C-IN.2:5

The Course is just one of thousands of spiritual paths, yet the illusory nature of this world is a foundational teaching of very few. It remains, however, a foundational teaching for *Course students* to take on! Ken Wapnick recalls an incident with Helen Schucman:

I remember on one occasion that Helen and I were with someone who was prominently associated with the Course, but did not really know what it said. Helen said to him that he would never understand this course unless he recognized that this world is an illusion. She was very emphatic:

'This world is an illusion. God had nothing to do with it, and you will not understand this course that way.'

Again, no one understood this course better than Helen.

The Course Manuscript History

Kenneth Wapnick (single quotes added)

Accepting the illusory nature of the world makes the Course clearer. But the real key to comprehending the Course is understanding that it is a purely non-dual thought system. And non-duality is the underlying principal behind the illusory nature of the world!

Here is a brief outline of non-dual thought:

* non-dual Reality has no parts that make it up
* non-dual Reality has no opposite
* non-dual Reality is the only existent Truth or Actuality

From these principals, it is easy to understand that the separated world is just a "seeming," a dream, an illusion! The Course teaches:

God does not know of separation.

P-2.VII.1:11

The world of our perception cannot be God's Reality as it is made entirely of parts. Also, this world cannot be "inside" God, as this would require that all the parts of this world be included as God's Reality. "We" dream! This dream, as any dream, is a real experience, but of something that never happened. You surely will agree that this dreaming is quite compelling! Pinch me, somebody! That's the trouble, isn't it? In this world curriculum of learning, a good "pinch" just seems to be evidence that the dream is real!

The acceptance of a non-dual Reality is helpful for Course students. Consider the following quote:

Each hour that you take your rest today, a tired mind is suddenly made glad, a bird with broken wings begins to sing, a stream long dry begins to flow again. The world is born again each time you rest, and hourly remember that you came to bring the peace of God into the world, that it might take its rest along with you.

W-PI.109.6:1-2

Beautiful passages such as these are part of the reason that many are attracted to the Course. This second sentence seems to contradict our earlier quote about the world! It is not a contradiction if we recall that the Holy Spirit meets you where you are, and that it operates in such a way as to *not* increase your fears. This, also, must be true of the Course.

If you are sure that the world *is not* an illusion, the second sentence seems like proof! If you are sure the world *is* an illusion, then here is proof for you also! In both cases, there is comfort. That is, perhaps, the real lesson. For those that understand the world as real, the passages provide an optimistic recognition of the mind's power to effect good and beautiful results in the world.

To know that there is no world is to understand that the world I look upon is the one I made up. A peaceful mind, therefore, beholds a peaceful world. Beholding a peaceful world comes from training my mind. This process is not about changing the world (not that there is one, anyway). As I fulfill my purpose, (changing my mind about the world that I made up), "the world is born again." This does not mean that God has given me something to "do" in the world or even that this world is not an illusion. It means I am waking up and waking up is my purpose.

Projection makes perception. The world you see is what you gave it, nothing more than that. But though it is no more than that, it is not less. Therefore, to you it is important. It is the witness to your state of mind, the outside picture of an inward condition. As a man thinketh, so does he perceive. Therefore, seek

> *not to change the world, but choose to change your mind about the world. Perception is a result and not a cause.*
>
> T-21.IN.1:1-8

More to the point, the purpose of a student of the Course, is as follows:

> *The sole responsibility of the miracle worker is to accept the Atonement for himself.*
>
> T-2.V.5:1

To "accept the Atonement for yourself" means to let go of all the barriers you hold in your mind against Love's presence. Each "letting go" is the *miracle* referred to in the Course. This is the process that forgiveness fosters. Without barriers, there is no dream of this illusory world, only the experience of eternal God-presence. As there *is* no world, the Course must be about the state of your mind and your thinking and not about getting what you think want in this world! (The Course is also *not* about *not getting* what we think we want in this world.)

In Science of Mind, the world is a real place that responds to what the mind is thinking. The goal is obtaining the "Good" of God by aligning one's thoughts with that Good. The emphasis is on "right" thinking in order to have the "right" result in the world.

In the Course, the world responds to the state of your mind (the barriers you hold) and not *what* you are thinking. The Course is not about changing what happens in the dream but waking up from it.

I am not saying that there is something wrong with accepting a literal reading of the lovely passage above. Read that way, it says that you came to bring peace to the world! There is nothing wrong with this interpretation. It just is not what the Course is teaching. This is not to suggest that the Course is right and Science of Mind is wrong. All spiritual practices are *maps* of a terrain and not the actual terrain. I *am* saying that a literal reading is more consistent with a map of a real world. If you let go of the literal meaning, the Course describes your *experience* of the world/illusion.

Per the Course, the Holy Spirit meets you where you are. Perhaps, believing the reality of this world is required for *your curriculum.* Or, perhaps it is important to *your curriculum* that your brother believes the world is real and you do not. *Your* question must always be, "Holy Spirit, what is your lesson for *me*?" *A Course in Miracles* might not be for you. Science Of Mind might be for you.

The "illusory nature of the world" idea can be a very challenging one. If we Course students are honest, most of us struggle with it. For example, one very significant pitfall is the incorrect thought that if the world is an illusion then so must I be! We think that word "illusion" means the same as "doesn't matter." This is also *not* what the Course teaches.

> *There are decisions to make here, and they must be made whether they be illusions or not.*
>
> **S-1.I.2:4**

The Course teaches that waking up from the illusion depends on the relationship you have with it. In the previously-noted quote from Helen Schucman, we see that there has been difficulty with this concept from the beginning. There is evidence that some our most well-known Course teachers struggle with this teaching. And, NO, there will be no names here! What they wrote, is what they wrote!

I am suggesting that this challenging distinction is a learning tool for the Sonship. It is unnecessary to try to homogenize either of these spiritual practices so that they conform to each other. Ultimately, the Course requires we look past the *form* these practices take, so that we may apprehend their *content.*

The Science of Mind community is one that has provided a safe and loving harbor for seemingly aliens, the Course community, whose beliefs and practices are not the same. The support of the SOM community is well appreciated in the Course community. It is the type of generosity that truly understands that giving and receiving are the same.

To both communities:

> *Forgive your brother all appearances, that are but ancient lessons you have taught yourself about the sinfulness in you. Hear but his call for mercy and release from all the fearful images he holds of what he is and of what you must*

be. He is afraid to walk with you, and thinks perhaps a bit behind, a bit ahead would be a safer place for him to be. Can you make progress if you think the same, advancing only when he would step back, and falling back when he would go ahead? For so do you forget the journey's goal, which is but to decide to walk with him, so neither leads nor follows. Thus it is a way you go together, not alone. And in this choice is learning's outcome changed, for Christ has been reborn to both of you.

T- 31:II.9:1-6

Rev. Ken Davis is a certified, professional lifestyle management coach, since 2006, whose focus is expanding spirituality as a basis for furthering life and business goals. His coaching is based on *A Course in Miracles* and Energy Leadership and he has authored a blog, ACourseInOnenessBlog.com. He was ordained in 2015 from the All Faiths Seminary International in New York. He can be reached at www.KenDavisCoaching.com.

Section IV

Individual Thinkers

Chapter 18

Rudolf Steiner

Harriet Sternberg

Although Rudolf Steiner made many contributions to the world in the arts (color, architecture, sculpture, painting), biodynamic farming, agriculture, nutrition, religion (the Christian Community), medicine, drama, dance, movement, economics, eurythmy, music, science, and social sciences, his works are not well-known by the general public. Educators may know him somewhat better as the founder of the Waldorf School Movement (with over 1000 in the world today). Steiner was born in February 1861, in Kraljevec, Austria-Hungary. Until the time of his passing in 1925, he produced some 35 written volumes and 4,500 to 6,000 lectures. Although highly influenced by the Theosophists and active in that belief in the late 1890s and early 1900s, he left their society in 1912 and founded his own. He called his teachings Anthroposophy. He established headquarters in Dornach, Switzerland; still today this is the center of the world-wide Anthroposophical Society and the School of Spiritual Science.

In order to make a comparison with *A Course in Miracles*, it is important to understand the basic concepts underlying Anthroposophy. "Anthroposophy is a path of knowledge to guide the Spiritual in the human being to the Spiritual in the universe. It arises in man as a need of the heart, of the life of feeling, and it can be justified only inasmuch as it can satisfy this inner need. Anthroposophy communicates knowledge that is gained in a spiritual way. Yet it only does so because everyday life and the science founded on sense-perception and intellectual activity lead to a barrier along life's way—a limit where this life of the soul in man would die if it could go not farther" (from *Anthroposophical Leading Thoughts: Anthroposophy as a Path of Knowledge: The Michael Mystery*, translated by George and Mary Adams, p. 13).

Many of the following Steiner comments are quite in contrast or opposition from those in the Course. Steiner was a believer in Christianity, viewing it overall as having a very positive, unifying influence for humanity. He stated Jesus' coming into the world was the greatest appearance on the Earth "...causing a truly decisive turning point in human history" (from *The Christian Mystery*). He gave a series of lectures (now a book title) on "The Reappearance of Christ in the Etheric." Also he wrote and spoke about the Mystery of Golgotha (Jesus' birth, death, and resurrection), the Lord's Prayer, John's gospel, the Sermon on the Mount, and Old Testament writings.

The Separation

The Course: Because of a "tiny, mad idea" the Son of God "forgot to laugh" and believed he could separate from God and Heaven. This is an illusion, a dream, and never really happened. *Steiner:* Reincarnation allows man to come to Earth in a planned way throughout various periods of time in order to evolve and perfect himself. Steiner often uses the expression, "In the life between death and a new birth...," then explains that in this interim period man works on becoming more self-conscious and resolving karma. In each incarnation, man is helped by various spiritual beings (from the Seraphim down to the Archangeloi). Whereas the Course emphasizes the role of the Holy Spirit or Jesus, Steiner stresses the saving help given over time by Archangel Michael. He refers to this age as "The Age of Michael." He also writes about two beings, Lucifer or Satan, and Ahriman, who sometimes help, but who also try in many ways to hinder man's development. This hindrance could be compared to the ego in the Course.

The Nature of Man

The nature of man is commonly referred to as a combination of mind, body, and spirit. The Course, however, is very specific in declaring that man is not a body. These statements tell clearly why not: *"I am as God created me. I am his Son eternally... This is the Self that never left Its home in God to walk the world uncertainly."* (W-p.I.3:3-4,7). *"At no single instant does the body exist at all"* (T-18.VII.3:1). In contrast, Steiner views man as having a body that has very special qualities and aspects: an ether or etheric body in common with the plant and animal kingdoms and the bearer of the forces of growth, reproduction, and nurture; an astral body, the seat of all desire, passion, and impulse; an

"I" ego body. The "I" identifies man's individual being, as does the ego, but the "I" is viewed also as God's name, as in the "I AM." The "I" transforms part of the astral body to become the Spirit Self. "A man has just so much of Spirit Self as he has created by his own efforts out of his astral body" (from Western Esoteric Masters Series: Rudolf Steiner, edited by Richard Seddon, p. 25). Furthermore, Steiner envisions the whole universe as having contributed to the building of man's overall body, "Man's physical body was prepared on Saturn; on the Sun was added the etheric or life body...on the moon was added the astral body and on Earth the ego..." (Ibid., p. 29).

The Ego

The Course is very clear and specific about how to view the ego. However, in many writings in the world, the ego is defined as both divine and worldly, part of the human personality. Since the ego refers to a self, it is easy to see why there could be confusion. The Course and Steiner agree that the human ego, or egoism, can cause problems for mankind in the world—attacks, conflicts, clashes, disturbances, competition, pain, poverty, distress, sufferings, and fears. Steiner suggests the ego should be worked out of or overcome while the Course states the ego is unreal, therefore, is to be disbelieved, forgotten, released, reinterpreted, or corrected. The Course states the following about the ego: it is a belief about ourselves made after the so-called separation; it has no knowledge and, therefore, no being; it regards the body as its home and uses the body for attack, pleasure, and pride; it causes us to see ourselves as tiny, vulnerable, and afraid; it wants us dead; it prevents us from recognizing our brother as he is in truth; it is a confusion in identity; although logical, it is clearly insane; it is never satisfied; it focuses on time and the past.

Steiner views the human ego as being both positive and negative—having an "I" which has evolved over eons of time to its present stage. Rather than citing the ego as an identity itself, Steiner is more likely to speak about man's egoism as having been a negative influence causing "bad people" and even some who do not grow to revert back to being animals. Egotistical beings focus on their own self-interest and neglect to serve the world or contribute to its progress. The Course states that the world does not exist, *"Therefore, seek not to change the world, but seek to change your mind about the world"* (T-21.in.1:7). This does not preclude world service; however, the primary focus is on awakening *from* the dream of the world.

The World

Both sources state there is another world other than the one we seem to perceive and to be in presently. In Course terms, this is referred to as the "real world" and in Steiner's, as "a super-sensible world" to which our earthly world is connected. Both also express that there will be changes. The Course states this occurs in the eternal *now,* not a future time. *"The end of the world is not its destruction, but its translation into Heaven"* (T-11.VIII.1:8). Steiner notes, "the effects of earthly existence will unite with what happens in this other world, giving rise to the new cosmic being into which the Earth will eventually be transformed" (from *An Outline of Esoteric Science*, translated by Catherine E. Creeger, p. 377).

As with other topics, the Course is very clear about the world that we made and adjust to, as not being God's world. The world we made is described as being chaotic, insane, merciless, having no meaning, and stressful. It believes love is impossible, tries to prove guilt is real, is full of violence and hate and, ultimately, does not exist. Steiner states both human and cosmic evolutions occur in the world. He views Earth as an incarnation of an ancient planet and as having undergone prior planetary stages with intervening stages of spiritualization. He labels past, present, and future of the Earth as having Saturn, Sun, Moon, Earth, Jupiter, Venus, and Vulcan phases of evolution. Traditional science does not show us these things, rather, spiritual science based on super-sensible perception. Eventually, all will become love. The Course states that all is love right *now*, with no evolution necessary.

Although this writing has highlighted some major differences, great credit should be given to the author of the Course, Jesus, and to Rudolf Steiner for the contributions they have made—and are making—towards the advancement of mankind at this time. Both offer structured lessons and exercises, as well as many illuminating ideas to help all on the path home to God.

Harriet Sternberg is a long-time teacher of the Course. She is co-author of two books on Archangel Raphael, and a presenter at Mind, Body, Spirit Expos.

Chapter 19

Freudian Psychology

Sam Menahem, Ph.D.

Sigmund Freud was a great pioneer in the field of psychology. He introduced the importance of the unconscious in human behavior. He also formulated the ideas of id, ego and superego, eros, thanatos, resistance, transference, ego defense mechanisms, separation-individuation, and the importance of trauma in psychological problems. Freud was a physician, trained in neurology and psychiatry.

Working with another physician, Dr. Josef Breuer, he treated many women with so called "hysterical symptoms." These women were suffering from paralysis or blindness with no known organic cause. He developed the idea that by going into the patient's past and having them remember sexual traumas from early childhood, they could be cured of their symptoms. In his early years, he used hypnosis. However, he was a poor hypnotist and soon developed the *free association* technique. The patient was instructed to say anything that came into their mind. Eventually, they would remember the trauma and go through a cathartic abreaction (re-experiencing the emotion). This emotional catharsis was the cure. It was a very controversial treatment (in late nineteenth-century Vienna) but seemed to work in many cases. That was the practical side of his work. However, there was also a theoretical side, the creation of an entire metaphysical system called psychoanalysis. Psychoanalytic theory formed the backdrop for all later psychoanalytic therapy.

According to Freud, all human beings are energized by a powerful, unconscious energy called the "id." The id is really *das es* in his native German, meaning more literally *the it*. The id, he said, is a result of metabolic processes. In other words, it was a physical, instinctual energy, shared by all human beings, who were first and foremost, physical beings. The id is a powerful force, characterized by sexuality (eros) and aggression. Hence, young human beings want what they want, and they want it now! What they want is sexual pleasure and power—complete control of their physical environment.

Since both of these goals are unrealistic, the instincts need to be controlled. It is the parents' job to provide appropriate limits and teach the young child to control him or herself. The sexual and aggressive impulses are pushed down or *repressed* into the unconscious mind by the demanding superego (the parental admonishments). The urges don't really go away, they are just hidden and may emerge as symptoms or behavioral problems. Repression is an automatic process. Anything that is not automatically repressed is to be controlled by other defense mechanisms, especially denial and projection.

When we are caught being too aggressive or sexual, we deny it or blame someone else. However, the superego is a little harsh sometimes, and id impulses are very powerful, so a new part of the mind develops. He called this the "ego" (Greek for "I"). The ego is the conscious part of the mind that seems to be who we are. It is composed of both id and superego elements. It is the conscious mediator between these two powerful forces. It only wants to be aware of acceptable impulses and needs to defend itself from both id impulses or drives and superego demands for proper behavior. Thus, it needs defenses to keep this acceptable front in place while secretly gratifying wishes for sex and power. This conscious part of the self (ego) is always afraid. On the one hand, it is afraid of the powerful sexual id. On the other hand, it is afraid of the mean, punishing superego. Thus, the job of the ego is to mediate between the demanding, sexual-aggressive id and the harsh, parental superego.

Psychoanalytic therapy was originally an *id* therapy. As the theory developed though, it became an *ego* therapy. Freud stated that the goal of psychoanalysis was to develop a strong ego, to ease the id-superego battle and live successfully and happily in the real, physical world. He wrote, "Where id was, ego shall be." Psychoanalytic therapy was designed to develop a strong ego. The job of the ego, the part of the self we are aware of, is to pretend that we are good citizens, channeling the powerful instincts into acceptable means. A mentally healthy human being, according to Freud, would have many healthy coping mechanisms or ego defense mechanisms to protect it from id impulses and superego demands. The psyche contains id, ego and superego elements. The more elements we are conscious of, as egos, the healthier we are. We are primarily our conscious selves, egos. We, said Freud, are physical beings, living according to the dictates of the ego, which wants to be safe. Safety, to the ego, requires many techniques of keeping the other parts of the mind at bay and dealing with the demands of physical life, which is the only real thing.

There was no room for God or a higher power in this system. God, to Freud, was an illusion, a sort of super parent image that didn't really exist. Any mystical feelings of oneness were simply regressions to a prenatal state of physical oneness with the birth mother. Spirituality was reduced to an unhealthy regression to the womb, in order to control anxiety.

A Course in Miracles presents a very different view of reality and life—in many ways it is a complete reversal of Freud's beliefs. However, in one aspect, psychodynamics, it is very similar. The Course is a channeled book. It was written by the metaphysical Jesus or Holy Spirit and brought into the material world through Helen Schucman. It completely reverses Freud's view of reality. According to the Course, we are One with the godly energy. At some point, a *tiny mad idea* of separation arose (T-27.VIII.6:2). This thought of separation led to the delusion that we are separate from God and merely physical creatures. All guilt, fear, and anger are caused by this central delusion of humankind. This idea is completely the opposite of the Freudian notion that we are physical creatures, driven by instinctual physical energy and suffering from the anxiety of trying to adapt that overpowering energy to living in the real physical world. *Freud's reality is the Course's unreality.*

According to the Course, the ego is the enemy of peace. As long as we listen to the mad voice of the ego, we will never be happy. I believe the Course's ego is what Freud called the id, ego and superego combined. Regardless, according to Freud, the ego is who we really are. There can be no ego without a body. According to the Course, the body and the entire physical world are simply a dream, an illusion. How different can you get? Thus, Freudian metaphysics and the Course are diametrically opposed.

Yet, the psychodynamics of the Course bear a startling similarity to Freud. Let us delve a little deeper into that matter. Leaving aside the issue of the reality of the ego, all human beings need to be mindful of this ego and how it operates in the phenomenal world of separation. The Course is very clear that as long as we think we are separate egos, we are prone to deny and project the primary emotions of guilt, fear and anger. Guilt, says the Course, arises with the separation. It is very disturbing to be fundamentally guilty. In the Course, we are guilty of wanting to create our own world, independent of God's world. This guilt is so powerful that we need to deny it completely. But we are secretly afraid that God will find out about our separate inclinations and punish us—kill us!!! So to avoid this painful guilt and fear, we deny that there is a God. We deny that we are afraid. We deny that we are guilty. If anyone challenges our denial, we get angry, maybe even righteously indignant! We then live in a vicious circle of guilt, fear, and anger, which we must deny or find someone else to blame. Maybe we even blame God—if we believe in Him—or just the government, big business, the world, or cruel fate if things don't go our way.

Strangely, Freud had similar conclusions. However, he said we are afraid not of God's wrath, but of our sexual and aggressive instincts, which are unacceptable to society. We then try to control the instincts and are afraid others may find out we are really very selfish and driven by sex. Soooo… we deny our unacceptable impulses or blame them on someone else. To Freud, the unacceptable impulses have nothing to do with God or spirituality. For the Course, the unacceptable impulse is to be separate from God in the first place, which then leads to all suffering. The best a Freudian can hope for is a fragile peace between warring parts of the self, which must defend itself from others knowing its true intentions. For the advocates of the Course, there is a much more hopeful answer. It is called the Atonement.

We are instructed to turn inward in prayer and get guidance from the inner teacher or Holy Spirit. We will then be guided to total forgiveness. We will realize over time that we are really one with God. As we pray for a change in perception, we will notice that we are all one spirit, sharing in our source. The holy instant is when we realize this at-One-ment with God. We can then give up all fear—there is no death. There is only eternal spiritual life. What we thought was "life"—physical life—was just an illusion. We are eternal, loving and peaceful.

The nightmare is over. To Freud, we have to live within the nightmare, which is the only reality. Then we die forever and are extinct. To the Course, we wake up from the dream of guilt, fear, and anger to a wonderful, true metaphysical reality. Which one do you prefer? I think I'll study the Course!

Sam Menahem, Ph.D. is a psychotherapist, professor and author of three books, *When Therapy Isn't Enough: the Healing Power of Prayer and Psychotherapy*, *All Your Prayers are Answered*, and *The Great Cosmic Lesson Plan: Healing through Spirituality, Humor and Music*. He has been a Course student since the 1980s. www.drmenahem.com

Chapter 20

Quantum Physics

Lorri Coburn

Quantum physics is confusing, confounding, and convoluted. It indicates that our universe is upside down, and what we think we see is not reality. In fact, physicists are having a hard time determining what reality really is. At the subatomic level, particles can be in two places at one time, can pop in and out of existence, can be created out of nothing, and can communicate faster than the speed of light, as if they are reading each others' minds.

Pioneer physicist, Neils Bohr, said, "Anyone not shocked by quantum mechanics has not understood it." Likewise, students of *A Course in Miracles* are known for throwing their Course books across the room and swearing about its seemingly ridiculous message. The Course and physics tend to agree that the nature of physical reality is deceiving. However, they diverge on the ultimate nature of reality, because the Course states that physical forms *do not even exist and have never existed.* In the meantime, many physicists are still searching for a grand unified theory that will explain how the universe works.

This article is a brief overview of complex topics; therefore, it is necessarily incomplete. Leading physicists differ widely in their interpretations of quantum reality and new discoveries are being made constantly. The Course is also subject to interpretation, therefore, so are the ideas in this article.

To compare concepts, it is important to distinguish between how the Course defines "heaven," as opposed to the earthly level of form/matter. Heaven is changeless, formless, eternal love. Nothing but God/Love exists and there is no physical universe, no bodies, no planets, no form. It is pure non-duality, oneness with no opposite. However, we *perceive* that we live in bodies on planet earth, so the Course speaks to us as if those are real, while telling us that ultimately, they are not. On earth, there is duality—apparent choices to be made among opposites. Separation is the rule—separate bodies, separate nations, separate time periods, etc. Heaven is *outside* of time and space, and, according to the Course, time and space *do not even exist,* because "*Reality is ultimately known without a form, unpictured and unseen*" (T-27.III.5:2).

A Particle or a Wave?

What Albert Einstein saw in quantum physics experiments upset him so much that he spent the rest of his life trying to figure out the missing puzzle pieces. He never found them, and while physicists continue to search for a grand unified theory, all they keep getting are more and more questions. The Course tells us that the ego's dictum is "*Seek and do not find*" (T-12.IV.1:4), which can explain the endless exploration of a universe that does not exist.

Most of us have heard of the idea that a photon can be either a particle or a wave. The gist of quantum physics is that nothing in the material universe is set in stone. There is no fixed reality in our world *until we look at it,* and no specific basic building block of matter that acts in a predictable way. The basic light photon can act either as a particle or a wave, but not both at the same time. It exists as *potential* states of being and does not collapse into form until something observes it. Then it becomes a specific particle in a particular space and time.

This bothered Einstein, and he said, "I like to think the moon is there even if I am not looking at it." Einstein is also famously known for saying, "God does not play dice (with the universe)." Stephen Hawking, the present-day Einstein who has developed theories of black holes, answers, "Not only does God play dice, but....He sometimes throws them where they can't be seen."

Just as everything is a throw of the dice, once we observe one thing, other aspects related to it are changed. The Heisenberg Uncertainty Principle states that we cannot know the position and momentum of a particle at the same time. Once the position (space) is measured, then the momentum (time/speed) cannot be measured, and vice versa.

The Course makes numerous statements in alignment with the particle/wave conundrum. A basic premise of the Course is that there is no world and we are making up the world. Nothing is real *until we decide it is* by looking at it, or, as the Course would say, *choose to perceive it.* The Course tells us over and over that we only see a physical world because we want that *instead* of heaven/Reality.

> *I have invented the world I see. Projection makes perception. The world you see is what you gave it…It is the witness to your state of mind, the outside picture of an inward condition.*
>
> W-p.I.32.h; T-21.in.1:1-2, 5

A popular metaphysical idea is that we create our own reality through the law of attraction. The movie, *What the Bleep Do We Know!?*, uses the observer principle to suggest that we can decide what we want in life, visualize it, and it will show up, as we collapse the quantum wave potential. Even though the movie features physicists, most mainstream physicists scoff at this idea, stating that the observer effect only applies to the subatomic level and not to large things and events.

Some students of the Course believe that the Course teaches the law of attraction, and cite the statements, "*I **am** responsible for what I see. And everything that seems to happen to me I ask for, and receive as I have asked*" (T-21.II.2:3, 5). Other students interpret this differently, stating all events happened in the past, (but actually never happened) and the only choice is to view events from the perspective of the Holy Spirit or the ego. To choose among images in the world is to choose among illusions, and the Course advises us to "*seek not to change the world, but choose to change your mind about the world*" (T-21.in.1:7). Even the choice for the Holy Spirit's Voice is an illusion, but it's an illusion that leads to Reality.

> *In this world the only remaining freedom is the freedom of choice; always between two choices or two voices.*
>
> C-1.7:1

Another interpretation of the above passage is that all possible events and scenarios happened in "*the tiny tick of time*" in which we dreamed this world (T-26.V.3:5). There are an infinite number of images that can show up, depending on whether we have chosen forgiveness and love with the Holy Spirit, or separation and fear with the ego. The infinite number of scenarios corresponds with the many worlds interpretation of quantum physics. This theory states that every thought creates a separate universe where that thought takes form.

All thinking produces form at some level.

T-2.VI.9:14

Whatever interpretation we choose, what we observe determines what we see. All of the above interpretations—the law of attraction, having a choice between the ego's or Holy Spirit's perspective, or seeing different images when we forgive—reflect the observer principle. As physics shows us, and the Course agrees, there is no objective reality. However, the Course states that the world is *in our mind*, while physics keeps looking to an *outer* physical universe.

Time and Space

Einstein's Special Theory of Relativity showed that time and space are relative to the observer and are not fixed, objective realities. For example, if an object is moving at the speed of light, it will not age as fast as an object that is moving slower. If there are two young men in their twenties, and one becomes an astronaut and spends years in space traveling at high speed, when he returns to earth he will be younger than the man who stayed earthbound.

Einstein noted, "The distinction between past, present, and future are only a stubbornly persistent illusion." The Course is in agreement that time and space are relative, and goes further to state they are *completely unreal.* The Course says that we are actually looking backward in time at events that have already happened, and we only *perceive* that they are unfolding in time.

> *Time is a trick, a sleight of hand, a vast illusion in which figures come and go as if by magic. For we but see the journey from the point at which it ended, looking back on it, imagining we make it once again; reviewing mentally what has gone by.*

W-P.I.158.4:1, 5

One of the Course's stated goals is to abolish the need for time (T-5.12.4:1).

> *The miracle minimizes the need for time. The miracle substitutes for learning that might have taken thousands of years. The miracle shortens time by collapsing it,*

thus eliminating certain intervals within it. When you perform a miracle, I will arrange both time and space to adjust to it.

T-1.II.6:1, 7, 9; T-2.V.A.11:3

Oneness and Bell's Theorem

The Course and quantum physics are in agreement about the interconnectedness of all things, which the Course calls "oneness" and physics calls "entanglement." The Course states that what we do to our brother, we do unto ourselves.

A major physics principle is Bell's Theorem, which was designed to test whether particles could be discrete, separate objects, unconnected to the rest of the world. The experiments derived from Bell's Theorem have shown that particles are inextricably interconnected. *There is no separation*, which is a primary principle of the Course. For example, say a particle is split into its twin half, and one half is in New York and the other half is in Los Angeles. When the particle in New York changes the rotation of its spin, the particle in Los Angeles *instantly* changes its spin correspondingly. How does the particle in Los Angeles know what its New York twin did? This communication is faster than the speed of light and happens without any apparent physical message, as if reading each others' minds.

The Course states that our only problem is the belief that we have separated from God (W-p.I.79.1:4). It also states that "*minds are joined*" (T-18.VI.3:1) and "*all I give is given to myself*" (W-p.I.126.h).

The Big Bang

Just like particles can arise out of nothingness, physicists say the universe arose from nothingness. How is this possible? The Big Bang Theory suggests that a dense, hot core of matter underwent a massive explosion that produced the physical universe. While the theory describes *what* happened, it still does not account for the *origin* of the matter that exploded.

The Course says the origin of matter in the *seeming* big bang is "*the tiny mad idea*," a *thought* in the mind of the Son of God (T-27.VIII.6:2).

The thought was nothing and the resulting world was nothing. The apparent world emerged in "*the tiny tick of time*" (T-26.V.3:5), all events happening at once, rather than over billions of years as physics tells us.

> *You do not realize the magnitude of that one error. It was so vast and so completely incredible that from it a world of total unreality had to emerge.*
>
> T-18.I.5:2-3

Conclusion

The Course and quantum physics agree on the dubious nature of physical reality, while the Course goes one important step further to say that physical reality does not, and never has, existed. In the Course, Jesus finally reveals the mysteries that have puzzled us forever. When we finally realize that the world is not *out there*, it's only in our *mind*, all the puzzle pieces that physicists seek are made clear.

> *There is no world! This is the central thought the course attempts to teach.*
>
> W-132.6.2-3

In the Bible, Jesus says, "I have yet many things to say to you, but you cannot bear them now. When the Spirit of truth comes, he will guide you into all the truth..." (John 16:12-13). In the Gospel of Thomas, Jesus tells us, "Those who seek should not stop seeking until they find. When they find, they will be disturbed. When they are disturbed, they will marvel, and they will reign over all." In the Course, Jesus says:

> *There is nothing outside you. That is what you must ultimately learn, for it is the realization that the Kingdom of Heaven is restored to you.*
>
> T-18.VI.1:1-2

John Bell, of Bell's Theorem, said "that the new way of seeing things will involve an imaginative leap that will astonish us." Now *that's* where physics is onto something.

Lorri Coburn, MSW is the author of *Breaking Free: How Forgiveness and A Course in Miracles Can Set You Free.* She conducts workshops on ACIM and speaks at national Course conferences. She facilitates a Course study group and has had a weekly show on ACIM Gather Radio for several years. www.lorricoburn.com

Chapter 21

J. Krishnamurti

Theodore L. Kneupper, Ph.D.

Jiddu Krishnamurti's teachings are usually considered to have commenced in 1929, when he concluded a momentous talk by saying, "My only concern is to set man absolutely, unconditionally free." In that same talk, he also declared his independence from the Theosophical Society and dissolved the Order of the Star of the East that Theosophists had formed around him. They had considered him to be the anticipated "World Teacher" predicted by Helena Blavatasky. Thereafter, almost to the time of his death in 1986, he articulated the nature of the pathless land of unconditional freedom, which is one of living in complete awareness of Love and Intelligence, and what brings it about.

A Course in Miracles came into expression late in Krishnamurti's teaching career by way of Helen Schucman. She claimed she heard a "Voice" that she eventually concluded was Jesus of Nazareth. Although there is no evidence that Schucman or the Voice were familiar with Krishnamurti's teachings, when one looks carefully at the two, one finds many similarities in their central insights, although expressed quite differently. There are also important differences between them.

Similarities

1. The prevalent human condition of separation/fragmentation. A first similarity is in their views on what most humans actually experience. The Course refers to this as "separation," while Krishnamurti's term is "fragmentation." This seems best understood as a state in which people think of themselves as fundamentally different from others, primarily in terms of the idea each has of himself. Thus, they see themselves as fundamentally concerned with their own well-being, but generally fail to understand that one's well-being is intimately connected with that of everyone else.

2. This condition is rooted in ego. Both teachings hold that the basis of this belief in division is in the mind's acceptance of the idea of "ego" or "I" as primary. This is the core of what the Course calls the "self-concept" and Krishnamurti calls "self-image." Ego can be understood as a mental form through which a mind thinks of itself as occupying a limited portion of what is within perception. It has its own thoughts, memories, and feelings that are fundamentally not the same as those of others. Thus, for Krishnamurti what is most important or of greatest value is what pertains to the overall condition of one's thoughts, including memories, images and more abstract ideas, and one's feelings, which include both emotions and sensations.

In the Course, what Krishnamurti calls thoughts and feelings are referred to as perceptions. The ego's boundaries are primarily determined by those of one's own body. Whatever personal thoughts and feelings are predominant make up one's perception. These are experienced as positive or negative, pleasant or painful, or a mixture of both. The primary aim is to achieve positive experiences and avoid negative ones. This is the core of what is thought of as "happiness" and "unhappiness."

3. The formation of further false beliefs. From this basic ego-dominated perspective, one further develops several general beliefs that act as guiding principles for life. The central belief is in the importance of preserving oneself as an ego-bounded entity. But one also accepts the presence of other ego-entities, along with beliefs about their place within one's experience. A primary belief is that other egos can be useful for, or a danger to, obtaining one's happiness. Thus, one regards others with ambivalence: some are drawn near, forming what are, in Course terms, "special love relationships." Others are regarded fearfully, as actually or potentially threatening, and may become "special hate relationships."

For Krishnamurti, both of these are described as simply "no relationship," since they involve not having an actual relationship with anything or anyone, but only a constructed image or illusion of what one calls "another." From this, a mind further develops beliefs about the larger collection of other ego-entities, forming what can be called "circles of special love and hate." Special love circles are the various social groups it thinks of as its community, church, nation, religion or ideology-sharers. Special hate circles contain its various "enemies," which are those belonging to groups outside of, competing with, or opposed to its own circles of special love. Both circles are fundamentally illusory for both Krishnamurti and the Course.

4. An alternative to the separated/fragmented mode of thinking/feeling living. However, both the Course and Krishnamurti teach that the mode described above is not the only mode that one can be in. As the Course puts it, there is "another way," and as Krishnamurti asks, "Is there an entirely different way of living?" The Course speaks of this as "living in the real world;" Krishnamurti as realizing "you *are* the world." Thus, both teachings propose that each person dominated by the ego-idea can undergo a process through which he clearly understands the actual truth of what he is, rather than remaining in the self-devised and generally conflict-filled state.

This process of transformation or radical change is called "Atonement" by the Course and "real revolution" by Krishnamurti. First let us consider the essential features of that process as viewed by the Course. What is essential is called "forgiveness." This term refers to a complete "letting go" of all false perceptions, including most beliefs that the mind has accepted. That process begins with the ego-dominated mind's decision to find "another way." This is based on a "little willingness" that this may occur. The second important step is that this little willingness moves toward being open to listening to the guidance of a higher Mind, called "the Holy Spirit." This term can be understood as a level of awareness deep within one's own mind that understands precisely what is necessary to do in each moment, so as to complete the transformation both within oneself and others. This is the essential move of what are called "miracles."

As the process proceeds, false perceptions due to ego-based beliefs are dissolved and replaced by true perceptions. Thus, the mind comes to listen more continuously to the Holy Spirit, so that it eventually completely unites with that Mind. As the Atonement reaches full maturity, what comes into awareness is the perception of "the real world." This is the full recognition that its "little self" is actually one with every other person, indeed, with everything it had thought itself as separated from. Within that awareness, which contains only true perceptions, there is a radical shift from being greatly limited and dominated by the notion of time to a fundamentally new mode, called "the holy instant," which is beyond time. Further, all relationships formerly viewed as special love and hate relationships are transformed into "holy relationships." There is complete awareness of the unity of oneself and all others, including those one had thought of as human and non-human.

Krishnamurti's teaching on the process of transformation, though different in description, seems substantially the same as the Course's. The real revolution begins when the ego-dominated mind recognizes its fundamental insufficiency in living. This occurs when that mind engages in "inquiry," calling into question all that it has accepted as true and observing closely all that arises in awareness. Engagement in inquiry is also called "meditation." This is not a matter of following some procedure prescribed by anyone else. Rather, it is opening the mind to permit the light of "Intelligence" to illuminate all of its thoughts and feelings. This involves giving full attention to "what is," that is, to all aspects of thoughts and feelings that arise each moment.

Although this may be helped by listening to the words of others engaged in meditative inquiry, such as Krishnamurti, it is fundamentally a process that can only happen within one's own ego-limited mind. The important thing is that, as one learns to inquire, by carefully and closely observing "what is," there arises a state of constant inquiry/meditation. In that state, all that is perceived and felt is illuminated by Intelligence. Thereby, the full meaning of all observed is made clear and all action undertaken is in harmony with all that is. The central feature of that fully transformed state of the real revolution is full understanding of the truth of the statement "I am the world," or "You are the world." In that state, as in the perception of the real world, the mind no longer operates in terms of past and future, but is in a mode completely beyond time, or simply in the "now."

Differences

1. The origin of separation/fragmentation. The Course teaches that separation arose due to a choice made in the mind of the originally perfect creature created by God, which it calls "the Son." This choice focused its awareness on limited aspects of reality, and persisted in that choice by fashioning an ego-idea and other limited ideas and beliefs. That is, separation occurred within an originally non-physical mind. Krishnamurti, however, offers no such metaphysical explanation. He places the origin of the fragmented mode within the context of an early period of human evolution, when it took what he calls "the wrong turn." He does not teach that there was an original non-physical mode of existence, although he does hold that our concept of time was entirely absent originally.

2. The role of "help" in undoing the separation/fragmentation. Another difference is in their views on how the problematic state is corrected. The Course teaches that the individual separated mind is quite incapable of achieving the transformation on its own, because its awareness is dominated by the belief in ego. It has constructed for itself a kind of mental prison from which its fundamental commitments prevent escape. Thus, it needs the help of a Mind outside that prison, the Holy Spirit, Who serves as its Guide and Teacher to instruct it regarding what it must do in order to be freed.

Krishnamurti, however, seems to dismiss the need for the help of any other mind, either human or higher—even Krishnamurti's own help—although he does observe that "Intelligence" has an important role. Transformation occurs only when one recognizes that dependence on any other person is completely futile. His view can be understood as calling for the fragmented mind's coming to complete congruency with Intelligence. His teachings give little detail about the operation of Intelligence, while the Course offers a wealth of insights about the activity of the Holy Spirit.

3. The final state. A further important difference is their views of the ultimate final state that is realized from transformation. The Course calls this "Heaven" or "the Universe of Love." (T-11.I.5:10). This state goes beyond the experience of the real world. All perception, which is intrinsically a limited mode of awareness, completely ends and is transmuted to a totally different mode, which is called "knowledge." This is a return to the original awareness in which the mind was created, which includes awareness of its Source, or God, and of its own unlimited and perfect creations.

In contrast, I have found nowhere in Krishnamurti's teachings any indication that there is such a trans-perceptual mode. However, this does not necessarily mean that he denies such a final state. Indeed, there are subtle indications, such as his speaking of one's coming to absolute Silence, that this may be the eventual final state. Perhaps, like the Buddha, he avoided trying to describe it, since no words are adequate, and any ideas that our minds might form about it are fundamentally illusory.

Of course, there are other similarities and differences between the two teachings that space limitations do not permit me to discuss here. However, what has been presented appear to me their major points of convergence and divergence.

In considering these similarities and differences, I close with two observations. One is that Krishnamurti's teaching was essentially focused on the possibility that our minds can realize something quite beyond the conflictive and fear-filled mode they are accustomed to, as well as the urgency to do so. This is the radically different mode of perceiving and living, which is implicit in "you are the world" and what the Course calls the real world, which involves the realization of perfect love as the primary quality. The other is that Krishnamurti's teachings can be seen as a kind of precursor to the Course's. He pointed out the importance of becoming free of all illusions that the ego-dominated mind invents, which prevent Love from operating with full freedom and ever-growing beauty. Indeed, I have personally found studying Krishnamurti's teachings to illuminate the Course's, and the study of the Course leads to much deeper insights into his teachings as well. In that sense, they can be seen as complementary.

Theodore L. Kneupper, Ph.D. is a professor emeritus of Slippery Rock University of Pennsylvania, where he taught philosophy for 34 years. He has studied the teachings of the Course and Krishnamurti for more than 30 years. In 2015 he published a scholarly inquiry into the Course's views on love, *'Love' in A Course in Miracles*. theodorekneupper@gmail.com

Chapter 22

Edgar Cayce

Judith Sherbenou

Edgar Cayce, a 20th century psychic, is undoubtedly the most carefully documented seer of his time. He gave more than 14,000 readings while unconscious, most of which were for physical illness and problems. Those who followed his advice experienced healing on many levels. Often, during a reading for a physical problem, he directed the inquirer to examine mental attitudes and spiritual concepts which may have contributed to the physical condition. Many of these ideas were incorporated into *A Search for God* books that were developed for group study. Many groups meet weekly across the USA and around the world to discuss and practice the teachings that came from Cayce. I have met with such groups for nearly 40 years. There is no "graduation date" for this type of study, as the individual grows spiritually through application and understanding. The same material studied in the beginning of a quest will take on deeper and more profound meaning as the student grows in consciousness.

Many Cayce students have expanded their study of the metaphysical to include *A Course in Miracles.* I obtained my first set of the Course books in the late 1970s and began reading them with great enthusiasm. Not wanting to let go of my Cayce studies, I attempted to see the Course as giving the same message. In many ways it does not. Yet, in some areas it *expands* the view presented by the Cayce material.

One obvious area of difference is in our physical "reality." Since most of the Cayce readings were given for physical problems, the Course's teaching that the physical world is an illusion presents a potential dividing line between the two. The attention we give to our physical bodies and materiality while we believe we are living in what the Course calls "the dream" can keep us from recognizing that we are still a part of God. Both Cayce and the Course teach that we remain connected with one another. Cayce would say the connection is at the super-consciousness level. The Course teaches that separation is an illusion. The differences here may not be as great as assumed. In one reading, Cayce said, "You are not your brother's keeper. You *are* your brother." Similarly, the Course states that there is only one son—and we are it (the Sonship).

Another area of difference between the two teachings is in the story of the beginning of the human race. According to the Course, the one Son of God had a "*tiny mad idea*" that it could separate from God—an idea at which he forgot to laugh (T-27.VIII.6:2). This resulted in the birth of the ego, which made all that we see and experience in the material world. Since God didn't create materiality, it is, therefore, an *illusion*. Our task is to wake up to this drama and realize that we have never left God.

Cayce, a devoted Bible student throughout his life, expands on the biblical story of Adam and Eve by revealing that the souls who left God-consciousness, through curiosity and willfulness, first entered the bodies of animals on earth. Forgetting their origins, they became entrapped. The so-called Sons of God were those who had not fallen into this trap. Amelius, as a consciousness, developed a way for these souls to be released to experience materiality through a body designed for such use—the first Adam. Since that time, those fallen souls have been reincarnating to learn and grow in consciousness and return to God. In Cayce's words, our goal is to "know ourselves to be ourselves, yet one with God."

According to Cayce, Jesus (who was also the first Adam) was the first to complete the trip. He was "Christed" when he returned to God-consciousness. Therefore, He is the pattern we must all follow to complete the experience and realize Oneness with God. Just as the soul known as Jesus required several incarnations to reach full awareness, the Cayce material indicates that we all utilize reincarnation as a learning tool. What we do to, or give to, others may manifest in a future life either as a challenge or a blessing.

In the perspective of the Course, God created only that which is true and real, both of which are changeless. Though Jesus is seen as the first to awaken from the dream, all of God's creation is the "Son of God." The Sonship was given the power to create but only as God would. The Son has misused this power by projecting. This happens when he perceives some lack and attempts to fill it with his own solution, rather than truth. When he is projecting, he is in the ego. The so-called "fall of man" is the mistaken belief that man is capable of separating himself from God. Since this mistaken thinking can only be corrected in the now, the Course emphasizes the present moment, disregarding the past or future. Reincarnation is not utilized to explain life's conditions, as man can only work out his salvation *now*. Though the Course mentions that we might return again and again, no experience in the illusion is considered to be real.

One area of agreement in the philosophies of the two teachings is the importance of forgiveness. Both teach that loving our brother does not allow for judgment. When we judge, we are declaring that there is something wrong with our fellow being and we are seeing him or her as separate—both from ourselves and from God. During this experience of judgment, we are coming from fear rather than love. The Course suggests that when we find ourselves doing this we pray, "Holy Spirit, help me see this differently." Cayce gave a powerful prayer, "Father, do that which is necessary to bring peace and harmony between us." Both of these prayers require that we release our need to be *right* and allow Love to prevail. The Course asks the question, "*Do you prefer that you be right or happy?*" (T-29.VII.1:9). Forgiveness requires that we release the need to be right—superior, more powerful, etc. "*Forgiveness is the key to happiness*" (W-p.I.121.h).

Cayce's view of karma emphasizes the value of forgiveness. He revealed that many times we find ourselves surrounded with those souls we've been with in the past. Some will be there to support us. Others may be in our lives because our inability to forgive them has forged an ironclad connection. Only when we have forgiven them will we be free. However, when we *have* done the forgiving work, we may find that we have no need to be free from them. Love may prevail.

Meditation is seen in the Cayce readings as vitally important to the spiritual awakening and growth of the individual. Prayer was defined as talking to God and meditation as listening to God's response. Daily meditation was recommended—preferably during the early morning hours when little interference would occur. The Course doesn't often use the term "meditation," but seems to recommend the practice when it talks of beginning each day by spending time with God. The student is also told to end the day the same way. In addition, the affirmations that head the daily lessons make an excellent focus for meditation.

Cayce encouraged the use of prayer, both for forgiveness and for healing the body and mind. He saw prayer as a means for attuning to God. Since the effect of our prayer is conditioned by our attitude, attunement with our spiritual source is essential for the most effective prayer. The Cayce readings often remind us to live as we pray, as our thoughts are prayers. The longer a thought is held in mind, the more powerful it is. Cayce believed that prayer or thought can be as powerful as a beam of white light. Prayer is not telling God what to do, but is a sending forth of spiritual energy to support the persons prayed for so that it will be available to them when they are ready to use it. He recommended praying for healing, forgiveness, attunement, and for the deceased. Most Cayce study groups keep an active prayer list.

The Course states that as long as perception lasts prayer is appropriate. Prayer is called the "*medium of miracles*" (T-1.I.11:1). However, the only meaningful prayer is for forgiveness, as those who have been forgiven have everything. The Course foresees the end of time and the end of the need for the dream world when the past has been fully forgiven.

The teachings that came through Edgar Cayce help us to live our earth lives in the most loving and healing way. Those of the Course show us that we can graduate from the dream of earth life by *withdrawing our belief that it is in any way real.* From this brief visit to the idea of combining the teachings of Edgar Cayce and those of *A Course in Miracles*, you are, hopefully, encouraged to continue in your endeavors to heal yourself by learning to forgive, love, and be willing to awaken to your place in the Oneness.

Judith Sherbenou is the author of Edgar Cayce and *A Course in Miracles*, published by the A.R.E. Press. For a more in-depth visit to the teachings of both philosophies, see this book. She is a retired teacher with a Master's degree in Education. Judith has been a student of the Cayce material for more than 40 years and a Course student since the late 1970s, shortly after the Course was published. jsherbenou@comcast.net

Chapter 23

The Seth Material

Sam Menahem, Ph.D.

For me, books are a blessing. From the time I spent six months confined to bed as a nine-year-old to the present, I have been entertained and enlightened by books. If I were marooned on a desert island like the characters in the TV show "Lost," I would want two books, *A Course in Miracles* and *The Nature of Personal Reality* by Jane Roberts (Seth). At first glance, these two books seem to be very different approaches to enlightenment. Upon further inspection, however, I feel that the two authors have more in common than meets the eye. Either philosophy, if utilized as an integral part of one's life, will have great benefit. This article will explain the similarities and differences between these two fountains of wisdom.

Dr. Sam Meets "Seth"

I encountered my first Seth book at the Paramus Park Mall, shortly after moving to New Jersey in 1977. I was browsing through Brentano's books, waiting for my wife, and decided to explore the "Occult" section. I was looking for laughs and picked up the silliest title I could find. "Seth" qualified and I began to read until my wife came in and announced that she wanted to go home. Instead of returning the "silly" book to the shelf, I bought it. I was off the next day and became so absorbed that I read the book in one day. Here is the philosophy that shook my reality then, in one sentence: "You create your own reality, through your beliefs, conscious and unconscious, period. There is no other rule."

Wow! That seemed right, but were there no exceptions? No, there were no exceptions. Seth, who describes himself as "an energy gestalt, of aware-ized energy, not presently focused in physical reality," presented this truth to Jane Roberts, a freelance writer from Elmira, New York. It seems that Roberts would frequently go into some sort of spontaneous trance, speaking of life from the spiritual perspective of a character named "Seth." Through Jane's mouth, Seth tells us that "We are much more than we think we are." In fact, we live many lives, on many levels, simultaneously. This is Seth's idea of reality and it also explains reincarnation.

Seth says that our many lives are all connected and happening at the same "time." Time, as such, does not really exist. We are actually multi-dimensional beings, living, loving, learning, and growing in an abundant joyful, loving, safe universe. Our purpose in this universe is to become aware of our responsibility for the kind of life we are living. As we become aware of our role in manifesting physical reality, we become aware that the physical is just an outward picture of *All That Is*, or *God*. Our perceptions and the seeming diversity is the result of our beliefs. So, in other words, there is a *Spiritual Oneness* (All that Is). The psychological beliefs then shape the one spiritual energy into the physical world.

I quickly realized that Seth was expressing a cognitive psychology (then in its infancy) and taking it to the "nth" degree. Our lives are simply a result of learned beliefs. Thoughts and emotions flow from these beliefs, not the other way around as most people think. As Seth clearly states, if you don't like your life, change your beliefs. Your life will then change, both in its physical manifestations and more importantly in your perceptions of everything in your life. Thus, he exhorts his readers to become consciously aware of their beliefs and change them. He has a four-step process for belief change: recognize them; face them; pull them out by the roots; replace them with more positive ones. Once I read Seth, I realized that my job as therapist was to help people by helping them explore their beliefs and teach them how to replace them with more positive beliefs. In other words, all our perceptions and feelings are results of beliefs. Change your beliefs and your perceptions change. If you want to heal your life on any level, just change your belief system.

To me, this explanation seemed nearly flawless. The only problem was implementing it. How can we control our entire life experience? How can we zoom in on what beliefs need to be upgraded and change them? How can we tackle the plethora of unconscious negative beliefs that might make us ill or bring on unfortunate events? The answers are all there in the Seth material. We need to trust our emotions and impulses. As we feel an emotion like anger, fear, or guilt, we need to allow it, recognize it as something that is flowing to us through our beliefs, and then tap into the power of All That Is to transform the beliefs and ultimately our lives into something better. Life will gradually appear to be better as we realize we have the power and ability to direct the "enlightenment" process. We are warned, however, to be patient, as there is a "time lag" in outpicturing the new beliefs.

To Seth, enlightenment means lightening up. He encourages us to playfully explore reality, until we realize the happy news that life is really great!!!! He calls the body "a living sculpture." He says that bodies are the best possible organization of cells and organs that can be accepted by the (fearful) ego at any time. It is the nature of the ego to resist change. Illness is an impeding action of the ego, a last-ditch effort of sorts to preserve everything the way it is out of fear of ego dissolution. However, if we listen to the message of the illness or symptom, we will be able to transform our belief system and heal the psychological problems (fear, anger, guilt) and the physical manifestations of the emotional problem. The emotions and or the symptoms are simply opportunities to heal what really needs to be healed—the belief system and the mind. As we heal, life becomes more joyful, abundant, creative, and loving. We lose all interest in being victims and become conscious co-creators of our lives with All That Is. This is only a brief synopsis of the Seth philosophy. Students of the Course may have already seen many similarities. Let us now turn to my other favorite source of wisdom, *A Course in Miracles.*

A Course in Miracles

After several years of studying and implementing the Seth material, I felt I had made substantial progress in life. Yet, I was always looking for something more. Thus, I was very curious about a new channeled book called *A Course in Miracles.* This book was not authored by some anonymous spook like Seth. This was allegedly written by Jesus, in order to correct the misinterpretations that were being espoused by orthodox churches. When I heard that the Open Center in New York was offering the Course, given by Diane Brook Gusic, I naturally signed up. Once again, I was enthralled. The book began with a dictum, "This is *A Course in Miracles*. It is a required course. Only the time you take it is voluntary" (T-in.1:1-3). I knew there was something special here from the get-go.

The miracle was so simply defined as the maximum amount of love that can flow through any individual. Great, I thought, now how do I open up to the love? Again, there was a simple answer, forgive everyone for everything, for in actuality, nothing really happened. Come to peace with the people in your life. Give up your righteous indignation and choose peace. How do I give up the need to be right all the time? Again, the answer is simple, turn to the *Holy Spirit*, the inner teacher. Pray and ask for guidance as to how to proceed. Ask the Holy Spirit to change our perceptions so that the seeming conflict can become a win-win situation. The change in perception is the true healing that allows the love that is there to flow. This is the peace of God, flowing through individuals. At a deep level, we will perceive that we are all part of the whole, extensions of a loving God.

We need to interact with others to come to this knowledge of peace, love, and joy. We need conflict to learn and grow. As we conflict with others, anger, fear, and guilt will come up. We then turn to the Holy Spirit or higher Self, asking for guidance, resolution, a change in perception. Each time we turn inward for guidance we will become more peaceful. There will be less pressure, less attachment to any particular result. We will learn to view human behavior as simply a call for Love or an extension of Love. We can then choose to release the blocks to love—anger, fear, and guilt. The more we become non-judgmental and let go of painful emotions, the easier it will be to forgive. We forgive, not because we are superior but because we are all part of the same One Spirit, God.

There is a reason we are continually tempted to judge and condemn others. It is called "the separation." At some point, we were at complete Oneness with God. Then, "a tiny mad idea" appeared. We thought we separated from our Source. This inevitably led to guilt. We think we shouldn't have done that and will be punished by our "Father," God. This creates fear, primal fear. We, of course, do not want to be guilty and afraid, so we often become angry instead. We then think we are helpless victims of other people, situations beyond our control, and even of God. We think that we are being punished for daring to be separate. These three emotions go around and around in the mass hallucination known as the physical world. This mass illusion is then taken as ultimate reality because the ultimate illusion, *the separation*, is too much to fathom. Thus, the psychodynamics and metaphysics of the Course point to the solutions. The solution is to withdraw our projections from others, forgive everyone because we are all one with the Source (God) and be peaceful, loving, and joyful. Salvation comes from accepting the Atonement (at-One-ment).

This system, like the Seth material, seems deceptively simple. Both systems recognize the main difficulty. The problem is the *ego*. The ego is the enemy of peace. The ego will fight tooth and nail to preserve the status quo. At first, the resistance will be intellectual. Many people think the Course seems too Christian. How can you forgive everyone? What about Hitler? Later the ego turns vicious. Tremendous fear may erupt. The body may get sick. Nothing is beyond the ego's need to maintain control, to preserve the status quo. I put the Course down for fifteen years after my students at Columbia University rated it as the weakest lecture in my course on non-traditional therapy. It just seemed too other-worldly, in denial of the physical world, and impractical. Needless to say, I have reversed my position. After nearly dying of heart attack five years ago, I picked it up again. I did all 365 lessons in one year. Then I started again. I re-read the text and read it again. I practiced the lessons daily. Finally, I began to favorably integrate it with my earlier Seth learnings.

Two Systems, One Message

At first glance, the Seth material seemed to be more accepting of physical reality than the Course. Seth tells us to joyfully, playfully accept physical reality. All we need to do is trust in All That Is and work on positive belief change. Seth tells us that the conscious mind can help us, but directs us toward belief change. The Course doesn't see the conscious ego as that benign or helpful. The ego will lead us astray. It is the inner teacher, the Holy Spirit that needs to direct our growth. At one time, the Course seemed to be saying to me that the unreal world (physical reality) needed to be ignored to be transcended. This is not what I now understand. Instead, very similarly to Seth, we are being told by the Course to use our experiences (anger, fear, guilt) and transform the conflicts leading to these emotions into peace. Seth says we do this by belief change. The Course says we do this by praying to the Holy Spirit for guidance, letting go of the need to be right and recognizing that we need to forgive others and ourselves by realizing that we are all One in God.

We need to change our perceptions of external events. Both systems see life as a process of evolving from tormented individuals to joyous beings of light. The joy emerges as we change our beliefs (Seth) and our perceptions (Course) from separation to wholeness. We change from thinking we are nothing but bodies with egos into knowing that we are holy children of God (Course) or endlessly creative, multi layered, joyous emanations of All That Is (Seth). Both systems see that energy is prior to matter. In fact, matter is unreal (Course) or simply one aspect of a multi-leveled "allness" (Seth). No matter which system you prefer, know that life is meant to be a joyous experience. We are spiritual beings in human form. The more we accept this "spiritual cognitive shift," the happier we will be.

Sam Menahem, Ph.D. is a psychotherapist, professor and author of three books, *When Therapy Isn't Enough: the Healing Power of Prayer and Psychotherapy*, *All Your Prayers are Answered*, and *The Great Cosmic Lesson Plan: Healing through Spirituality, Humor and Music*. He has been a Course student since the 1980s. www.drmenahem.com

Chapter 24

Mother Teresa

Miradrienne Carroll

One of my clients was stalled in her healing because she had not yet begun to practice forgiveness from the vantage point of forgiving illusions. She flopped back and forth from cool denial to abject misery in the knowledge that she had been abused for 41 years. We explored her present and her past, released emotional backlog, prayed, refilled with peace, love, and self-worth, and spoke of projection many times. However, she continued to manufacture more pain because her underlying judgment of herself and others didn't budge. In order to nudge her into peace and hand her the steering wheel for her emotions, I wanted her to learn to retrieve her projections with wide-open eyes. But when I tried to teach her a fool-proof method for taking back her projections, she revolted.

A devout Catholic, she was convinced that the principle upon which true spiritual forgiveness is based—the unreality of perception because it is based on our projections—is against her religion. The God of her understanding rewards sacrifice and punishes the guilty. She could not condone doing otherwise, and so ended counseling with me.

Within hours, I came across some writings of the candidate for Catholic sainthood, Mother Teresa. Look at the resonance of Mother Teresa's message with the Course in this excerpt from *In the Heart of the World*, "On Silence" (with ACIM passages following in italics and brackets):

> "In the silence of the heart God speaks. If you face God in prayer and silence, God will speak to you. Then you will know that you are nothing. It is only when you realize your nothingness, your emptiness, that God can fill you with Himself…" [*I call upon God's Name and on my own* (W-p.I.183.h). *I choose the second place to gain the first* (W-p.II.328.h)].
>
> "We cannot put ourselves directly in the presence of God if we

do not practice internal and external silence." [*Let me be still and listen to the truth* (W-p.I.106.h)]

"In silence we will find new energy and true unity..." [*I rest in God. The world is born again each time you rest...*(W-p.I.109.h; 6:2)]

"Silence of the heart is necessary so you can hear God everywhere..."[*God's Voice speaks to me all through the day* (W-p.I.49.h). *All things are echoes of the Voice for God* (W-p.I.151.h).]

"To make possible true inner silence, practice:

* Silence of the eyes, by seeking always the beauty and goodness of God everywhere, and closing them to the faults disturbing to the soul." [*Be vigilant only for God and His Kingdom* (T-6.V.C.h).]

* "Silence of the ears, by listening always to the voice of God and to the cry of the poor and the needy, and closing them to all other voices that come from fallen human nature, such as gossip, tale bearing, and uncharitable words." [*Let every voice but God's be still in me* (W-p.II.254.h).]

* "Silence of the tongue, by praising God and speaking the life-giving Word of God that is the truth, that enlightens and inspires, brings peace, hope, and joy;" [*God's peace and joy are mine* (W-p.I.105.h).] "and by refraining from self defense and every word that causes darkness, turmoil, pain, and death." [*In my defenselessness my safety lies* (W-p.I.153.h).]

* "Silence of the mind, by opening it to the truth and knowledge of God in prayer and contemplation..., and by closing it to all untruths, distractions, destructive thoughts, rash judgments, false suspicions of others, vengeful thoughts, and desires." [*Peace to my mind. Let all my thoughts be still* (W-p.II.221.h).]

* "Silence of the heart, by loving God with our heart, soul, mind, and strength; loving one another as God loves; and avoiding all selfishness, hatred, envy, jealousy, and greed." [*God is but love, and therefore so am I* (W-p.I.Review-V.4:3).]

"I shall keep the silence of my heart with greater care, so that in the silence of my heart I hear His words of comfort, and from the fullness of my heart I comfort Jesus in the distressing disguise of the poor." [*I give the miracles I have received* (W-p.I.159.h).]

"For in the silence and purity of the heart God speaks." [*In quiet I receive God's Word today* (W-p.I.125.h).]

One of the most sacred sites I know is the ecumenical chapel of a large cancer hospital where I do massage therapy. The energy of this small space carved out for prayer and meditation is strikingly sweet and still. Amidst a swirling mass of stress, fear, and pain mixed with love, dedication, and hope, this tiny oasis radiates the presence of God. A squash-orange banner announces through symbols the parade of religions honored in the chapel: Native American, Wicca, Goddess, Hinduism, Taoism, Judaism, Buddhism, Christianity, Islam, Confucianism, and several more I don't recognize.

It is certain that these religions do not agree in theology, yet the space dedicated to all of them exudes peace and unity. Every time I pause in this chapel, I remember that we are unified by the God we seek, not by our particular beliefs about It. *Perception is a mirror, not a fact* (W-p.II.304.1:3). My lost counseling client is my projection, mirroring the part of me that still believes in victimhood, guilt, and punishment. That she remains my bodywork client reflects the Christ nature—the unconditional practitioner of forgiveness—in both of us. We gently agree to disagree. And in the stillness of the chapel of my heart, I know we are One in God and closer now to *the holy place we never left* (W-p.II.234.1:1).

Miradrienne Carroll is a student of *A Course in Miracles*, a certified hypnotherapist, a licensed massage therapist and spiritual counselor in Houston, Texas. In this accelerated world she's already lived at least three lifetimes in the same body! The grateful guardian of a formerly feral cat who doubles as her muse, she is currently at work on her first novel. Mira is the author of *Healing Loss: Choose Love Now*. www.alohaservices.org; alohaservices@earthlink.net

Chapter 25

Sir David R. Hawkins, M.D., Ph.D.

David T. Bell

David Hawkins left the earth plane in 2012 at the age of 89. His life work was devoted to alleviating suffering as a result of erroneous thinking. After service in World War II, he worked his way through medical school and became a psychiatrist. At the age of 38, with a progressive, fatal illness that did not respond to any available treatments, in a state of extreme anguish and despair, he called out "If there is a God, I ask Him to help me now!" He surrendered to whatever was to be in store and went into a state of oblivion. Upon awakening, a transformation of such degree had taken place, that he was completely awestruck. There was no personal self or ego, only Infinite Presence of unlimited power. The miraculous happened. Many chronic maladies from which he had suffered for years disappeared, eyesight normalized, and radiant health appeared. As though on its own, a clinical practice resumed and became huge. There were two-thousand outpatients from all over the country. There were more than fifty therapists, a suite of twenty-five offices and many support staff. Patients came from all over the world, including some of the most hopeless cases.

The work became taxing and overwhelming. Enormous frustration over the seeming never-ending stream of seriously ill patients led to the study of the physiological response (muscle testing) to various stimuli. What was discovered was the lost connection with higher reality, the Divine. Through rigorous testing with the aid of students and research assistants, the discovery of the power of the mind and the creation of the map of consciousness led to the decision to leave the practice and New York City behind, in order to devote himself to a wider dissemination of these radical discoveries to mankind. After settling in Sedona, Arizona, the life of teacher, author and lecturer began. In the ensuing years, eleven books were written, hundreds of lectures given and many videos created, all with the goal of assisting mankind to transcend the ego, to re-establish the awareness of the Presence of

Divinity, and to thereby benefit the whole of humanity.

A major piece of the life-work of Hawkins is the discovery of the map of consciousness and the proposition that one could inquire into the truth or falsehood of any idea and could determine, through muscle testing, also called kinesiology, the level of truth of a teaching and the consciousness level of a teacher. The map is a numerical scale in which shame is measured at 20, and enlightenment occurs at 600. The higher realms up to 1000 are descriptive of great saints and avatars. Jesus, Buddha, and Krishna all calibrate at 1000. While this has no corresponding relationship with the Course, it is instructive and can aid in leading a student in transcending the ego. Hawkins spoke highly of the Course, and actually utilized the Workbook in conjunction with the technique of letting go, in healing his multiple serious illnesses. He relates the following in his book, *Letting Go:*

"At a certain point, both the mechanism of surrender and *A Course in Miracles* were investigated and applied to daily life. Because of the busy work schedule, there was very little time for any new techniques. Happily, the 'Workbook' of *A Course in Miracles* requires the simple contemplation of a sentence or 'lesson' throughout the day. The power of this technique is the elimination of guilt by utilizing the mechanism of forgiveness. The mechanism of surrender could also be done silently throughout the day as an inner process. The two tools worked together. Surrendering and forgiving went on simultaneously during the day" (pp. 302-303).

David Hawkins had several extraordinarily deep mystical experiences. These experiences were direct and radiant moments of the Presence. These experiences, some separated by decades of his life, imbued him with awe and love for Divinity. Each of his eleven books begins and ends with the expression "Gloria In Excelsis Deo." It could be fairly said that God, the experience of the Divine Presence, was the dominating goal of his life work. His goal, after leaving the psychiatric practice, was to alleviate suffering through the teaching of methods for transcending the levels of consciousness and the ego. All with a view toward impacting the largest number of people possible.

In his lectures and repeatedly in his books, he maintained that the single most important thing that one could do for all of mankind was to raise one's own consciousness. In other words, to practice extending love and forgiveness. This is consistent with Course principles such as "You are the savior of the world," and "Extending love is always the appropriate response."

In *Letting Go*, Hawkins includes an entire chapter on the importance of Love. There are numerous obvious parallels to the Course. In the following passages from that chapter, he echoes several Course principles. "Lovingness is a way of being that transforms everything around you because of the radiation of that energy. It happens on its own. We don't have to 'do' anything, and we don't have to call it anything. Love is the energy that silently transfigures every situation." This accords with the principle that *"(We) need do nothing"* (T-18.VII.h). It also is similar to the principle that "*...there are no private thoughts*" (W-p.I.19.2:3). This is seen in the energy field of love as a transformative power. The extension of love, even though no words are said, has an impact on any situation. Hawkins tells the story of an undirected flow of this energy in the autobiographical section of his books.

"Occasionally, an exquisitely blissful energy, an Infinite Love, would suddenly begin to radiate from the heart toward the scene of some calamity. Once, while driving on a highway, this exquisite energy began to beam out of the chest. As the car rounded the bend, there was an auto accident; the wheels of the overturned car were still spinning. The energy passed with great intensity into the occupants of the car and then stopped of its own accord. Another time, while I was walking on the streets of a strange city, the energy started to flow down the block ahead and arrived at the scene of an incipient gang fight. The combatants fell back and began to laugh, and again, the energy stopped." This is a classic example of the miracle of the extension of Love, being directed by the Holy Spirit, for the highest good of all concerned. It required the presence of a consciousness of a high-enough degree, such that the ego was virtually absent and the Self was fully present.

The author of this chapter has had the opportunity to test the premise of kinesiology on several occasions. Photocopies of pictures of Adolph Hitler and Mohandas Gandhi were inserted in plain envelopes, concealing the contents from view. Test subjects were invited to hold the envelopes, one at a time, against their solar plexus. In every case the envelope containing Hitler made the subject go weak, and the envelope containing Gandhi made the subject test strong. In some cases, the test subjects were completely befuddled by the results, and others simply said that the result made perfect sense. What is true about the results is the belief by the author that kinesiology is a valid method for determining truth versus falsehood and calibrating consciousness levels.

On one occasion, this author tested the above pictures of Hitler and Gandhi at an Interfaith service. Surprisingly, the subject, who was a student of the Course, tested strong on both pictures, unlike the previous subjects who had tested weak on Hitler. It was later read in Hawkins' book *Power vs. Force* that students of *A Course in Miracles* who had studied up to Lesson 75 no longer weakened with thoughts of Hitler, because of their awareness of humanity's oneness.

In speaking about the relationship of the mind and the body, Hawkins relates, "The mind with its thoughts and feelings controls the body; to heal the body, thoughts and feelings need to be changed." "The body is not the real self; it is like a puppet controlled by the mind" (*Letting Go,* p. 295). This is simply a restatement of Course principles. "All healing takes place in the mind." "*I am not a body, I am free. For I am still as God created me*" (W-p.I.201-220.h).

A well-known quote from the Course says: "*Love holds no grievances. When I let all my grievances go I will know I am perfectly safe*" (W-p.I.68.6:8-9). This is precisely the central theme of Hawkins' final book, *Letting Go*. His premise throughout the book is that negative feelings, including grievances, are the parents of all of our negative thoughts. This is slightly different from the Course in that the Course states that thoughts are the parents (cause) of all things, including the body's negative feelings. However, it agrees with Hawkins that dissipating the energy behind negative feelings is a tool to rid the mind of related negative thoughts. The mind that is free of negativity is the mind that can choose to listen to the "Voice for God." Such a mind is open to *true perception*. The technique of "Letting Go," as suggested by Hawkins, is an additional tool that aids the student in pursuing "A Course of Unlearning."

In the Course we read,

> *You must have noticed an outstanding characteristic of every end the ego has accepted as its own. When you have achieved it, it has not satisfied you. That is why the ego is forced to shift ceaselessly from one goal to another, so that you will continue to hope it can yet offer you something.*
>
> **T-8.VIII.2:5-7**

The penultimate paragraph in Hawkins' first book *Power vs. Force* is an accurate description of the same point, arrived at by an entirely different route. That however does not detract from its verity; it confirms the validity of both descriptions. That paragraph reads as follows:

"The ubiquitous human ego is not an 'I' at all; it is merely an 'it.' Seeing through this illusion reveals an endless Cosmic Joke in which the human tragedy itself is part of the comedy. The irony of the human experience is in how fiercely the ego fights to preserve the illusion of a separate, individual 'I' even though this is not only an ontological impossibility but the wellspring of all human suffering. Human reason exhausts itself ceaselessly to explain the inexplicable. Explanation itself is high comedy, as preposterous as trying to see the back of one's head, but the vanity of the ego is boundless, and it becomes even more overblown in this very attempt to make sense of nonsense.

The mind, in its identity with the ego, cannot, by definition comprehend reality; if it could, it would instantly dissolve itself upon recognition of its own illusory nature. It is only beyond the paradox of mind transcending ego that that which *Is* stands forth self-evident and dazzling in its infinite Absoluteness. And then all these words are useless."

This seems to capture the complete essence of the purpose and process of the Course. Yet Hawkins' approach was arrived at through scientifically verifiable methods of kinesiology rather than through communication with Jesus of Nazareth. Rather than seeking to determine which source is the "right" one or the "better," it seems that the concordance of two very different approaches, in the final analysis, lends even more credence to them both.

The Course tells us that when all ego interferences have been removed and there remains nothing left between God and us, God Himself takes the last step, lifting us unto Himself. This goal of all Course students is captured brilliantly in the final paragraph of the autobiographical section of each of David Hawkins' eleven books:

"But, in fact, in this final apocalypse of the self, the dissolution of the sole remaining duality—that of existence and non-existence—identity itself dissolves into universal divinity, and no individual consciousness is left to choose. The last step, then, is taken by God alone."

One is left then to exclaim, "*Gloria in Excelsis Deo!*"

David T. Bell has been a student of *A Course in Miracles* since 1983. He has led a study group since 1996. Ordained as an Interfaith Minister in 1998, he is a graduate of the New Seminary. He has led an interfaith congregation in Ann Arbor, Michigan, since 1998. He holds a BBA in Accounting from Western Michigan University, and a Juris Doctor degree from the University of Michigan. dave@interfaithspirit.org

Chapter 26

Adyashanti's Principles of Spirituality

Bonnie Nack Ed.D.

Adyashanti is an American born spiritual teacher who lives in California. Many of his lectures are available on You Tube. He teaches four basic principles of Advita, an ancient Hindu spirituality that echoes and compliments the teachings of *A Course in Miracles.*

Adyashanti's first principle is that suffering is caused by our identification with ego consciousness instead of being aware of our true nature. Human beings are caught in a collective state of egoic conscious which is the root of all suffering; whereas our true nature is "Consciousness Spirit."

Like *A Course in Miracles*, Adyashanti teaches that ego attributes suffering to factors outside of itself such as life circumstances and memories of past experiences. He goes on to explain that the ego's response to its environment causes it to create certain limited patterns of thinking and behaving. The consciousness conceptualizes these experiences and identifies itself with its limited patterns of thought. It believes them to be his own individual identity. Then ego spends a lifetime indiscriminately applying these concepts and repeating these patterns in other environments and with other people, and wonders why it experiences so much unhappiness and frustration.

Adyashanti's second principle is that ego is a creation of the mind; a conglomeration of beliefs and judgments which confirm that you are a separate being. This is the same message of The Course in Miracles. Addiction to this conglomeration of thought results in deep and profound suffering.

Our true nature cannot be found in the thoughts of the mind. Our true nature is the silent center of awareness that exists before thought. The Course calls this quiet state of mind Peace which is the goal of The Course.

Adyashanti goes on to teach that spiritual seeking is based on ego's addiction to thinking. Spiritual seeking is born of the ego and the seeking itself thwarts attainment of spiritual realization. Ego and all its thinking is the primary illusion that needs to be dispelled in order for you to come into a whole new realization of who and what you are.

It is necessary to recognize the unreality of what the mind is doing. In The Course, this is called the illusion. Thinking does not define anything. Thinking is something that happens *within* what you already are. It is necessary to recognize you are something other than the thoughts mind has created.

Adyashanti's third principle is that freedom from ego consciousness comes from awakening to what he calls, "Consciousness Spirit." This echoes the central question of The Course; "Are you a body or are you Spirit?" Both Advita and The Course teach that you are not the ego and its thought patterns; you are Spirit.

Ego is nothing more than a circular self-confirming pattern of thinking. Awakening is simply no longer believing or identifying with that pattern; identifying rather with "Consciousness Spirit," the silent awareness that exists prior to thought. You cannot escape ego by battling against it. The thinking mind must be eliminated. We are ineffable beings beyond what the mind can conceptualize. Spirituality is an awakening to that fact.

Adyashanti's forth principle is that when you have awakened, the values that guide your life are not like the moral values of this world. You no longer guide your life by values of this world, such as money, power, beauty, competition, control, punishment, revenge, etc. Awakened values are *inherent* in "Consciousness Spirit." They are Truth, Peace, Unity, Harmony, Happiness, Joy, Freedom, Gratitude and Love. These are *inherent* truths of "Consciousness Spirit." They are the essence of who and what we are; the fundamental goodness built into us and the world.

Awakening to "Consciousness Spirit" changes our perception and transforms our whole way of understanding and living in the world. This teaching echoes ideas taught in *A Course in Miracles*; seeing God in everyone and living your life under the guidance of the Holy Spirit.

Adyashanti goes on to provide three applications of his principles. The first is "Be Still." Allow everything to be just as it IS. Do not judge or try to control anything. Allow it to be in its natural state. As long as you resist anything, nothing will change. The Course also teaches non-resistance.

The second application is "Self Inquiry." This is the practice for finding your true nature. As you passively watch your patterns of thought and recognize their nothingness, Adyashanti teaches you will discover that more and more frequently your consciousness will move on the ground of Spiritual rather than moral values.

Your consciousness will become the place of ongoing revelation of Spiritual truths. The ongoing process of inner revelation is seldom taught by teachers of *A Course in Miracles*. In this culture we understand the revelations of God as insight and a deepening of understanding.

The last application is *awareness* of "Consciousness Spirit." What is awareness of "Consciousness Spirit?" It is ineffable; it has no shape or form. You cannot touch, taste or feel it. There is no concept or word that can name it. When you discover it, you become conscious that all along you have been it. You have merely been unconscious of it. It has been hidden beneath all your thinking.

Awareness of "Consciousness Spirit" gradually leads you to identify with God. When you are awakened you come to the realization that we are all one and the same "Consciousness Spirit." This, of course, echoes what the Course in Miracles calls Atonement; we are all extensions of the One Mind of God.

Bonnie Nack, Ed.D. is a retired psychologist who worked for 25 years in community mental health; the mother of two daughters and grandmother of three grandsons. She is the author of *Twelve Keys to Unlocking the Secret of Miracles in A Course in Miracles*. She is presently working on another book; a *User's Manual* for souls who find themselves in human bodies. BonnieNack99@gmail.com

Chapter 27

A Course of Love

Michael Mark

A Course of Love (ACOL) is a spiritual text received between 1998 and 2001 by Mari Perron, consisting of three volumes combined into a single volume: The Course, The Treatises, and The Dialogues. In addition to being received through the voice of Jesus, the work establishes its connection to *A Course in Miracles* (ACIM) in its very opening pages, where it is written in the Prelude of ACOL, "This is *A Course in Miracles*. It is a required course. The time for you to take it is now. You are ready and miracles are needed."

Students of ACIM will notice not only the parallel between these sentences and the Introduction of ACIM, but the subtle distinctions as well—distinctions that shift emphasis but are not necessarily contradictory. It is this shift in emphasis without contradiction that I find to be one of the beautiful hallmarks of *A Course of Love*.

Fundamental shifts embodied in the movement from ACIM to ACOL are the fact that it was written for the heart, that it describes a transition from indirect learning to direct revelation, that it focuses upon establishing our shared identity in Christ by which the end of learning is achieved, and that it inspires our heartfelt participation in the "creation of the new," which is all that will arise upon our return to the Heart of Creation as the ego and its attending fear are left behind.

A shift in emphasis is simply a response to changing conditions. New forms of response are appropriate when the conditions being addressed have changed, and ACOL is clear in noting that we live in a time when "readiness for miracle-mindedness is upon us," largely due to the work of ACIM.

It is also important to keep in mind that intellectual understanding is not the end sought in either work. The only outcome worthy of us, as Children of God, is the relinquishment of the ego and a return to unity with God—not as a concept, but as our complete and undivided experience of reality. Our concepts alone are simply not enough. I believe ACOL greets many of us at the point where we have committed to returning to Love's reality, but still are caught here and there by old patterns of the mind. Some shred of resistance remains in us, and we continue to suffer.

Both ACIM and ACOL have arisen in response to the needless suffering of the Children of God, and are self-described efforts to save time. The emergence of ACOL is neither a referendum on the validity of ACIM, nor on the validity of you and me. To see the emergence of the new as meaning there was something truly missing or lacking in what came before is to continue the mistake of misconstruing simple misperception as sin. No one is blameworthy here: it is simply the case that continued engagement is required to accomplish the learning outcomes desired.

One of the key shifts from the approach contained in ACIM to the approach contained in ACOL is that the latter is written for the heart. Whereas ACIM is self-described in its opening chapter as *"a course in mind training,"* ACOL is self-described in its Introduction as "a course for the heart," and in the Prelude as a means of "approaching this final learning through the realm of the heart."

The importance of the heart is acknowledged early in ACIM, where it says, *"where your heart is, there is your treasure also"* (T-2.II.1:5). This is further expressed in Workbook Lesson 164: *"There is an ancient peace you carry in your heart and have not lost"* (W-p.I.164.4:2).

One aspect of this shift to a heart-centered approach in ACOL is the introduction of the idea of wholeheartedness. While the heart and mind are both discussed in ACIM, often appearing in parallel expressions of a common idea and with hints of their relatedness, their unified condition is not directly discussed. Typical examples include: *"Let related thoughts come freely, for your heart will recognize these words, and in your mind is the awareness they are true"* (W-p.I.62.5:5); and *"In the quiet of my heart, the deep recesses of my mind, I wait and listen for your Voice"* (W-p.II.221.1:3). ACOL delves into this matter directly, however, as in the following passage: "A united mind and heart is a whole heart, or wholeheartedness" (ACOL C:17.17).

The wholeheartedness of ACOL is a further answer to the split mind that was described in ACIM. The concept of a split or conflicted mind is essential to both Courses, and is associated with the thought system of the ego. The importance of thought systems is also emphasized throughout both works, more than one may suspect in ACOL with its emphasis on the heart.

In ACIM the term "One-mindedness" is used in a way that is analogous to the wholeheartedness of ACOL. One-Mindedness is not defined directly in ACIM, but this passage from the fourth chapter gives a clear indication of its importance: *"Salvation is nothing more than 'right-mindedness,' which is not the One-mindedness of the Holy Spirit, but which must be achieved before One-mindedness is restored"* (T-4.II.10:1). One-mindedness is thus a word used in ACIM to denote the condition of a healed mind, and all that this entails.

While on the one hand it seems clear that One-mindedness and wholeheartedness are intimately related—and I believe they are—the symmetry in the terms belies one of the more significant shifts in emphasis contained in ACOL. This shift is a movement from a reliance upon the intermediary of the Holy Spirit—the Comforter and Guide who *"mediates higher to lower communication"* (T-1.II.5:3)—to a time of direct communion with God.

This is consistent with the shift from a focus upon the logic of the mind to the pure knowing of the heart. As ACOL says in the Introduction, "The mind is its own reality. You cannot escape the mind's reality with the mind. You cannot learn how to escape the reality of the mind with the mind's pattern of learning or of logic. You cannot live in a new and fresh world and retain the mind's reality" (ACOL C:I.9). In contrast, the heart "responds in love to what is one with it" (ACOL C:I.6).

It is this response to our reality in unity that Jesus wishes to awaken within us—the loving response of the created to their Creator. ACOL notes that, "Love is the only pure response of the created for the Creator, the only response of the Creator to the created" (ACOL C:1.1). This echoes a sentiment in ACIM, where Jesus says, *"Any response other than love arises from a confusion about the 'what' and the 'how' of salvation..."* (T-12.III.5:3).

This movement from indirect to direct means of knowing was envisioned early in ACIM, where it was noted that the time of the Holy

Spirit would pass as the Atonement is completed, but that the Holy Spirit would remain with us, *"to bless [our] creations and keep them in the light of joy"* (T-5.I.5:5). In another portion of this same passage the Holy Spirit is described as *"the Christ Mind which is aware of the knowledge that lies beyond perception"* (T-5.5:1). Taken together these passages presage a key development in ACOL, which is the establishment of our true identity in Christ. We no longer need the intermediary in the same way once direct contact has been re-established.

This shift to complete acceptance of the Christ within us represents a new pattern—a shift in emphasis to direct revelation. "The difference between this time and the time that has but seemed to have gone before has already been stated as the difference between the time of the Holy Spirit and the time of Christ. This has also been restated as the difference between the time of learning through contrast and the time of learning through observation. It is further stated here as the difference between learning by contrast and indirect communication and learning through observation and direction communication or experience. The same truth has always existed, but the choice of a means of coming to know the truth has shifted" (ACOL T:4.1.17).

In both Courses a very significant aspect of our identity in Christ is that it is a *shared identity* in Christ. In ACIM our true identity is referred to as being a shared one in various places, as expressed in this passage from the Workbook: *"In this equality is Christ restored as one Identity, in which the Sons of God acknowledge that they all are one"* (W-p.II.9.4:3). ACOL echoes this sentiment throughout, beginning in the Prelude where it says, "The Christ in you is your shared identity" (ACOL C:P.39).

But a shared identity can be scary to contemplate. A great fear described in both Courses, and related to the theme of releasing our false identification with the ego, is the fear of loss. We fear that in accepting a "shared identity" we will lose something valuable to us. We fear we will lose that intangible something that makes us each unique. While ACIM addresses this perceived loss of individuality to a limited extent by referring to the special function each of us is given, ACOL explores the topic of our existence as unique expressions of a shared identity to a considerable extent.

One of the first instances of this comes in a chapter entitled "The Embrace," a Chapter in the first of the three volumes of ACOL in which the shift in emphasis between the two Courses becomes obvious. In this chapter, Jesus says, "Expressions of love are as innumerable as the stars in the universe, as bountiful as beauty, as many-faceted as the gems of the earth. I say again that sameness is not a sentence to mediocrity or uniformity. You are a unique expression of the selfsame love that exists in all creation. Thus your expression of love is as unique as your Self. It is in the cooperation between unique expressions of love that creation continues and miracles become natural occurrences" (ACOL C:20.30).

This beautiful passage not only addresses the insanity of the fear we encounter when reflecting upon a shared identity, but reveals that our ability to express love *uniquely* is integral to the intended workings of creation. In fact, without the recovery of our true identity in Christ, and the setting aside of fear and the ego's thought system, it is not possible for us to reclaim the place that has been held for us in creation. Our place is never lost, but if we are to *experience* it, we must accept and *embody* our true identity as One in Christ.

This introduces one of the final shifts in emphasis to be explored in this article, and one of the more challenging to navigate for some ACIM students, which is the idea that physical creation and individual expression can, in fact, be transformed into living expressions of Love itself. To understand the way in which this is possible it is important to understand the way in which our relationship to the body shifts as our shared identity in Christ is accepted.

Early in ACOL the idea introduced in ACIM of the body as a learning device was re-emphasized. In ACOL the time of separation is equated with the time of learning, for learning is required while we still perceive falsely. With the acceptance of our true identity in Christ, however, the need for learning ends and is replaced by the fulfillment of our natural function as creators, in unity and relationship. This fulfillment will bring about the new.

In ACOL, Jesus says, "Like all that was created for the time of learning, the body was the perfect learning device. Seeing it as such assisted us in bringing about the end of the time of learning. But now your body—your form—must be seen in a new way. It is thus with new ideas about the body that we will begin the final thought reversal that will allow you to live in form as who you truly are" (ACOL D:6.5).

It is the importance of this idea of living in form as "who you truly are" that is perhaps the most significant shift in emphasis from ACIM to ACOL, for without the willingness on our part to express Christ consciousness in our lives, to embody it and to make it known, the new reality that we desire in our hearts cannot be born. And yet it is this marriage of spirit and form that is what we have so long desired. It is the end of duality.

The idea that we might "embody" who we are in form, without mistakenly identifying with the form as *all* that we are, is indeed a huge shift in emphasis. In ACIM, (speaking to minds deeply entrenched in the thought system of the ego), the point was made time and time again that a basic choice must be made to look upon the spirit instead of the body.

This passage from ACIM provides a typical example,

> *"The body is the means by which the ego tries to make the unholy relationship seem real. The unholy instant is the time of bodies. But the purpose here is sin. It cannot be attained but in illusion, and so the illusion of a brother as a body is quite in keeping with the purpose of unholiness... if you see the body, you have chosen judgment and not vision. For vision, like relationships, has no order. You either see or not."*
>
> **(T-20.VII.5).**

The intent of passages such as these is clearly to establish the idea that while our entire identity is mistakenly placed within the body, the purpose is sin. We cannot declare the body as our home without choosing separation from God and one another. To perceive clearly, we must see the timeless nature of spirit instead. ACOL supports the nature of these passages, which are written to teach a split mind, but ACOL also leads us to the frontier of creation that lies *beyond* the split mind. In Christ-consciousness, with our true identity restored, it is no longer possible to look upon the body with the purpose of sin. This is why the body is seen "in a new way."

ACIM presages this healed view of creation even in its first chapter, where Jesus says, *"'Heaven and earth shall pass away' means that they will not continue to exist as separate states. My word, which is the resurrection and the life, shall not pass away because life is eternal. You are the work of God, and His work is wholly lovable and wholly loving. This is how a man must think of himself in his heart, because this is what he is"* (T-1.III.2).

What does it mean for heaven and earth to no longer continue as separate states? I believe this is an early reference to the union of the two that is described in ACOL as creation of the new. In the Treatises, the second volume of ACOL, Jesus says, "There has always been a state of consciousness that we are here calling Christ-consciousness. There has never been a sustained Christ-consciousness in form" (ACOL T4:12.22).

Later in ACOL, Jesus goes on to say, "What then is the call to creation that has been spoken of? This is the acceptance of the *new you*—acceptance that you are going beyond simple recognition and acceptance of the Self as God created the Self—to the living of this Self in form. This is an acceptance that recognizes that while the Self that God created is eternal and the self of form as ancient as the sea and stars, the elevated Self of form is new and will create a new world" (ACOL D:5.15).

The elevated Self of form is the expression of Christ-consciousness within the universe of matter and form. Christ, as ever, is the bridge, and with the ego gone forever, and level confusion healed once and for all, it is possible to sustain Christ-consciousness even as this consciousness is expressed in form. It is possible to express who we are without mistaking our ever-changing expression with our eternal and unchanging nature. With our true identity restored, we will no longer interpret the physical world as *all* that we are, but as an integral aspect to our eternal existence in the One Heart of God.

As Jesus says in ACOL, "Matter is simply another word for content, and need not be maligned. The content of all living things is the energy of the spirit of wholeheartedness. The content of all living things is, in other words, whole. By seeing only aspects of wholeness you have not seen content nor matter truly. You have not been aware of all that you are. You are thus now called to discover and to become aware of all that you are. The body, rather than aiding you in learning as it once did, will aid you now in this discovery.

"Realize that this is a call to love all of yourself. You who once could love spirit *or* mind, mind *or* body—because of the dualistic nature associated with them—now can love all of your Self, all of God, all of creation. You can respond to love with love" (ACOL D:7.9-10).

It is this response that we were unable to give while shackled by the thought system of the ego. While conflicted and separated from one another, we were deprived of our freedom and power, and unable to will as One with God. We were unable to express the true nature given to us, and sought to forge natures of our own—natures that were falsely tied to matter, to the body, and to the egoic self.

We are left then where we knew we always would be, at the beginning.

"Creation of the new has begun. We are an interactive part of this creative act of a loving Creator. Creation is a dialogue. Creation—which is God and us in unity—will respond to our responses. Will respond to what we envision, imagine, and desire. Creation of the new could not begin without you. Your willingness for the new, a willingness that included the leaving behind of the old, a willingness that included the leaving behind of fear and judgment and a separate will, was necessary to begin creation of the new. Your former willingness to accept the old but kept creation's power harnessed to the old. Does this not make perfect sense when you realize that creation, like God, is not 'other than' who you are? How could creation proceed on to the new without you?" (ACOL T4:12.34).

The journey on which ACIM and ACOL both take us is truly "one without distance," one in which the experience of separation and our false identification with the ego is replaced with knowledge, and the attending experience of unity. We remember that we are One Heart, One Mind, and One Body in Christ. What lies beyond the restoration of our shared identity in Christ is the eternal and joyous expression of what is—of who we are.

Both Courses speak of this transition, though the emphasis in each is different. We see in the deep relatedness and movement of these two Courses an inkling of our own relatedness to our loving Creator. We begin to sense the nature of this holy dialogue that is creation, in which love responds to love and we are free to express forever and without end the joy that is our birthright, our nature, our inheritance and our home.

Michael Mark is a utility systems engineer and a writer who has published two collections of spiritually-themed poems. He also maintains a blog featuring his poetry, sporadic experiments with fiction, and the occasional Course-related piece at www.embracingforever.com. *A Course in Miracles* and *A Course of Love* have been two of the most significant influences upon the unfolding of his inner life. m.mark248@gmail.com

Section V

Therapeutic Programs

Chapter 28

Alcoholics Anonymous

Anonymous

Alcoholics Anonymous has many traditions, and one is that A.A. has no opinion on outside issues; hence, the A.A. name ought never be drawn into public controversy. Another is that anonymity is the spiritual foundation of all our traditions, ever reminding us to place principles before personalities. Therefore, I will only speak for myself anonymously and in no way am I representing A.A.'s opinion on any issue and, in particular, on *A Course in Miracles.*

A.A. and the Course are both based on ancient teachings, ideas and truths. They were both divinely inspired. In the case of the Course, Jesus dictated to Helen what to write exactly. In the case of the book, *Alcoholics Anonymous,* it was written by the group consciousness of the first 100 people that found sobriety. Both books brought to the world new ways for humans to relate to God and each other.

The Cause is in the Mind; The Solution is Spiritual

Most people go on a spiritual quest because they are experiencing pain or discomfort. I find it fascinating that both texts identify the cause of unhappiness as being *in the mind. Alcoholics Anonymous* notes that once an alcoholic takes a drink, he cannot stop and is in a hopeless situation: "We know that while the alcoholic keeps away from drink, as he may do for months or years, he reacts much like other men. We are equally positive that once he takes any alcohol whatever into his system, something happens, both in the bodily and mental sense, which makes it virtually impossible for him to stop. These observations would be academic and pointless if our friend never took the first drink, thereby setting the terrible cycle in motion. Therefore, the main problem of the alcoholic centers in his mind, rather than in his body" (pp. 22-23).

The solution for the alcoholic is *a spiritual experience.* This is explained as either happening quickly or over time but, "With few exceptions our members find that they have tapped an unsuspected inner resource which they presently identify with their own conception of a Power greater than themselves. Most of us think this awareness of a Power greater than ourselves is the essence of spiritual experience. Our more religious members call it 'God-consciousness'" (pp. 567-8).

The Course always stresses that the deceived mind needs to be undone. The Workbook lessons undo thoughts so the Holy Spirit can guide a willing participant.

> *Both miracles and fear come from thoughts. If you are not free to choose one, you would also not be free to choose the other.*
>
> T-2.VII.3:1-2

I find the Workbook lessons and the Twelve Steps of A.A. to be very similar in this regard. Both are a way to create ego deflation so that a new guide can enter. It is a *willing surrender*, usually brought on by many years of spiritual distress. Both are asking for a complete and all-encompassing change in perception.

> *The purpose of the workbook is to train your mind in a systematic way to a different perception of everyone and everything in the world. The exercises are planned to help you generalize the lessons, so that you will understand that each of them is equally applicable to everyone and everything you see.*
>
> W-In.4:1-2

The echoes of complete surrender are heard in recovery as well. In the paragraphs immediately preceding the Twelve Steps in *Alcoholics Anonymous,* one finds phrases such as, "If you have decided you want what we have and are willing to go to any length to get it—then you are ready to take certain steps...Some of us have tried to hold on to our old ideas and the result was nil until we let go absolutely" (p. 58). "Without help it is too much for us. But there is One who has all power—that One is God. May you find Him now!...Half measures availed us nothing" (p. 59).

New Concepts of God

One story in *Alcoholics Anonymous* describes the process of conceptualizing God differently: "Just before a co-founder of A.A.

stopped drinking, he was very anti-religion, having lost faith and developed an intelligent dependence on science. He paid a visit to a man who used to be as bad a drinker as he. The former drinker had changed so much that the man had to wonder if God had been the answer. He stated, 'I could go for such conceptions as Creative Intelligence, Universal Mind, or Spirit of Nature but I resisted the thought of a Czar of the Heavens, however loving His sway might be.' I have since talked with scores of men who felt the same way. My friend suggested what then seemed a novel idea. He said, 'Why don't you choose your own conception of God?' That statement hit me hard—it melted the icy intellectual mountain in whose shadow I had lived and shivered many years" (p.12).

Most adults experience hardships and disappointments. I found it very difficult to break from my childhood concepts of God. I was raised to believe God had a Son and that Son loved little children. I was also taught that God sent his only Son to save our sins. As a child, I would wonder, "If it is God, surely he can make another Son." It sure would relieve some of my guilt that God's *only* Son had to die for me. This is where the Course comes in and saves the day, because God did *not* ask Jesus to die for me.

> *If the crucifixion is seen from an upside-down point of view, it does appear as if God permitted and even encouraged one of His Sons to suffer because he was good. This particularly unfortunate interpretation, which arose out of projection, has led many people to be bitterly afraid of God.*
>
> **T-3.I.1:5-6**

Another sticking point throughout my adulthood was when I felt sadness or grief and prayed to God for help. I felt conflicted. I believed that God created this world and took people to heaven when He saw fit. He also did not prevent hurtful things from happening to me or to those I loved. How could I pray to a God that I believed caused the harm in the first place? Why would I believe He would be helpful now after being so mean before?

The Course concept that God does not know of this world was so healing for me. Now I *could* pray for help—not to get what I wanted, but for help and guidance. God no longer was a heartless entity that caused or did not prevent tragedy. God is Love and wants only Love for me.

The Cause of Pain Is Our Own

Alcoholic Anonymous gave me permission to choose a loving, caring God and the Course explained why that was true. This led me to ask, "Then why do I continue to feel pain from time to time?" This is another common thread of belief within the Course and A.A.—our pain is of our making. A.A. puts it this way in the book *Twelve Steps and Twelve Traditions:* "It is a spiritual axiom that every time we are disturbed, no matter what the cause, there is something wrong *with us*. If somebody hurts us and we are sore, we are in the wrong also. But are there no exceptions to this rule? What about 'justifiable' anger?…Nor were we ever skillful in separating justified from unjustified anger. As we saw it, our wrath was always justified" (p. 90).

The Course agrees that we are incapable of judging correctly.

> *In the end it does not matter whether your judgment is right or wrong. Either way you are placing your belief in the unreal. This cannot be avoided in any type of judgment, because it implies the belief that reality is yours to select* from.
>
> **T-3.VI.2:10-12**

If we are unable to judge then we literally do not know what is "good' or "bad" for us and, therefore, what pain or non-pain is. The Course further explains:

> *Whenever you are not wholly joyous, it is because you have reacted with a lack of love to one of God's creations. Perceiving this as "sin" you become defensive because you expect attack. The decision to react in this way is yours, and can therefore be undone.*
>
> **T-5 VII. 5:1-3**

The Happy Destiny and Happy Dream

An important focus of both AA and the Course is undoing ego and behaviors that are rooted in habit and deep beliefs. The ego must be brought to light, seen, and then discarded. This clears the way to join with our fellows. This is how both texts end:

"Abandon yourself to God as you understand God. Admit your faults to Him and to your fellows. Clear away the wreckage of your past. Give freely of what you find and join us. We shall be with you in the Fellowship of the Spirit, and you will surely meet some of us as you trudge the Road of Happy Destiny. May God bless you and keep you—until then" (*Alcoholics Anonymous*, p. 164).

> *Not one illusion is accorded faith, and not one spot of darkness still remains to hide the face of Christ from anyone. Thy Will is done, complete and perfectly, and all creation recognizes You, and knows You as the only Source it has. Clear in Your likeness does the light shine forth from everything that lives and moves in You. For we have reached where all of us are one, and we are home, where You would have us be.*
>
> **T-31.VIII.12:5-8**

Anonymous has been sober in A.A. since 1996 and has been a student of the Course since 2005.

Chapter 29

Alcoholics Anonymous

Rev. Ellyn Kravette

This is A Course in Miracles. It is a required course. Only the time you take it is voluntary. Free will does not mean that you can establish the curriculum. It means only that you can elect what you want to take at a given time. The course does not aim at teaching the meaning of love, for that is beyond what can be taught. It does aim, however, at removing the blocks to the awareness of love's presence, which is your natural inheritance. The opposite of love is fear, but what is all encompassing can have no opposite.

T-IN.1:1-8

This is the truth. All else is the journey Home to the authentic self through the disengagement of the myriad illusionary pathways we have created.

As I compare the Steps of Alcoholics Anonymous and the Course, there are some things I would like to share about my pathways, my perceptions, and my authority to accomplish this task. My personal journey has led me to be influenced not only by Alcoholics Anonymous but by the Course and many other religious, spiritual, psychological and ultimately, psycho-spiritual paths. I have been gifted to be able to hear the beauty and truth in many walks of life and many ways of thinking. My heart acknowledges all as we each bring our own personal experiences to an all-encompassing experience of God. My ideas are not original and I have noted teachers whose ideas have impacted my thinking. Further reading of any of their works is a good idea. No person is authorized to speak for AA, so this sharing is of a personal understanding. I accept that I am a conduit and that divinity flows through us all and so I open my heart to reveal a path of illusion and homecoming that I and many others have been privileged to walk.

Addiction is a biopsychosocial dis-ease which impairs normal functioning. It is a combined genetic and stress-induced defect in the midbrain and prefrontal cortex dopamine and glutamate reward system. It results in symptoms of decreased functioning including: loss of control, craving, and persistent use despite negative consequences. Due to its chemical impact through the body, memory, pleasure, choice, and learning systems are impaired. Acting from a biological "fight or flight" perception, addicts come from and create a social system that is crisis-centered, reactive, negative, fearful and consequently disappointing, angry, wounded, and wounding.

In this atmosphere of impulsiveness, distrust, and woundedness, love and the experience of abuse or insatiable neediness are often confused, even though there may be a longing for love. Attachments shaped by anxiety, the threat of insecurity, and fear result in settling for an immediate illusion that creates a sense of control, soothing, or relief from anxiety. This toxic pseudo-solution reinforces a sense of depravity and unworthiness.

Codependency is simply another manifestation of the addictive system. It appears as an indiscriminant hunger for appreciation or affection, an obsessive concern with approval and a contradiction between the wish for love and the capacity to feel, receive, or give love. Whether one is addicted to a substance or to an addictive relationship, there is a retreat to something toxic, self-defeating, and inherently incapable of providing a healthy attachment. There is an illusion of not being dependent when one is addicted to a substance, or an illusion of being in relationship when one is actually codependent. Addiction blocks the ability of the real self to consciously and pro-actively relate physically, emotionally, and spiritually to life. The illusion continually falls apart, leaving one exhausted or "sick and tired of being sick and tired." Therefore, its recovery must be addressed physically, emotionally, and spiritually, thus, providing a rich and fertile soil for the acceptance of a miracle.

Step One: Alcoholics Anonymous

We admitted we were powerless over alcohol—that our lives had become unmanageable.

TWELVE STEPS AND TWELVE TRADITIONS

In the First Step, the alcoholic/addict admits the reality that their life has become *unmanageable* and that a *toxic substance controls* them. This admission begins an exploration because "there must be a different way" than the world of desperation. The addict is not powerless to make choices but accepts that they are powerless over a toxin which impairs their ability to make a choice. Without a drug they would not choose this system of chaos, which is created to obscure the truth of their addictive system.

The Course Text: Reversing Effect and Cause

> *This world is full of miracles. They stand in shining silence next to every dream of pain and suffering, of sin and guilt. They are the dream's alternative, the choice to be the dreamer, rather than deny the active role in making up the dream. They are the glad effects of taking back the consequences of sickness to its cause. The body is released because the mind acknowledges "this is not done to me, but I am doing this." And thus the mind is free to make another choice instead. Beginning here, salvation will proceed to change the course of every step in the descent to separation, until all the steps have been retraced, the ladder gone, and all the dreaming of the world undone.*
>
> T-28.II.12:1-7

Step Two: Alcoholics Anonymous

> "Came to believe that a Power greater than ourselves could restore us to sanity."

Addiction is a choice for victimization and enslavement. Step Two tells us that there is something outside of the deluded self which can give us the ability to function in moral context with deliberation.

The Course Text: Beyond All Symbols

> *A power wholly limitless has come, not to destroy, but to receive its own. Give welcome to the power beyond forgiveness, and beyond the world of symbols and of limitations.*
>
> T-27.III.7:2,8

Step Three: Alcoholics Anonymous

"Made a decision to turn our will and our lives over to the care of God *as we understood Him.*"

This Step opens the door to the possibility of trusting. It represents a major shift for someone whose expectations have been consistently negative. It reminds me of the story Henri Nouwen and Sue Monk Kidd tell in With Open Hands of the woman whose fists were constricted as she held on to the only thing she possessed in this world. When the fists were finally opened, it was discovered that what she was holding on to were pieces of garbage. The risk of letting go of her only possession was overwhelming and so she was starving, unable to let go to use her hands for anything else except holding on.

Likewise, the addict, and often their family, hold on to the chaos they know—the pain that has become familiar. It is more desirable than the fear of uncertainty and its potential to be worse. Consequently, asking the addict to turn their will and life over to the unknown is huge. This Step, once taken, affords the unbinding of the limitations of addiction. The experience of living can now begin to flow.

The Course Text: The Healing Example

Accept the miracle of healing, and it will go forth because of what it is. It is its nature to extend itself the instant it is born. And it is born the instant it is offered and received.

T-27.V.1:2-5

Step Four: Alcoholics Anonymous

"Made a searching and fearless moral inventory of ourselves."

Taking Step Four, a searching and *fearless* moral inventory, allows the addict to "fear less." As in the treatment of post-traumatic stress disorder (PTSD), perceived injuries, disappointments, angers, and instances of abuse are acknowledged. Defense mechanisms become clearer as patterns of behavior are revealed. Self-understanding and acceptance are the keys to separating from the diseased self and begin the process of getting in touch with the authentic self.

The Course Text: The Healing Example

> *If you wish only to be healed, you heal. Your single purpose makes this possible. But if you are afraid of healing, then it cannot come through you. The only thing required for healing is a lack of fear.*
>
> T-27.V.2:5-8

Step Five: Alcoholics Anonymous

> *Admitted to God, to ourselves, and to another human being the exact nature of our wrongs.*

To allow someone else to see our shame and guilt through their loving eyes is the true spirit of confession and reconciliation. As the addict has begun to heal through Steps 1, 2, 3 and 4, looking back objectively, the nature of the illness becomes clearer, the need for self recrimination dissipates and the ability to choose wellness (wholeness) is demonstrated.

The Course Text: The Self-Accused

> *Only the self-accused condemn. As you prepare to make a choice that will result in different outcomes, there is first one thing that must be overlearned. It must become a habit of response so typical of everything you do that it becomes your first response to all temptation, and to every situation that occurs. Learn this, and learn it well, for it is here delay of happiness is shortened by a span of time you cannot realize. You never hate your brother for his sins, but only for your own. Whatever form his sins appear to take, it but obscures the fact that you believe them to be yours, and therefore meriting a "just" attack.*
>
> T-31.III.1:1-6

Step Six: Alcoholics Anonymous

> *Were entirely ready to have God remove all these defects of character.*

One of the problems inherent in the concept of forgiveness in many religions is the need to forgive without first owning or admitting, even to the self, the extent of our anger regarding real or imagined hurts. One cannot give up what they do not possess. Relinquishing attack requires a process that leads to the refusal to maintain negative thoughts or actions. Realizing that there is no "need" to defend or attack, the addict can relinquish their defense mechanisms and replace them with compassion.

The Course Text: The Savior's Vision

> *Have faith in him who walks with you, so that your fearful concept of yourself may change. And look upon the good in him, that you may not be frightened of your "evil" thoughts because they do not cloud your view of him. And all this shift requires is that you be willing that this happy change occur. No more than this is asked. On its behalf, remember what the concept of yourself that now you hold has brought you in its wake, and welcome the glad contrast offered you. Hold out your hand, that you may have the gift of kind forgiveness which you offer one whose need for it is just the same as yours. And let the cruel concept of yourself be changed to one that brings the peace of God.*
>
> **T-31.VII.5:1-7**

Step Seven: Alcoholics Anonymous

"Humbly asked Him to remove our shortcomings."

Note simply that the willingness work was a step by itself, prior to the "letting go" step.

Steps Eight and Nine: Alcoholics Anonymous

> *"Made a list of all persons we had harmed, and became willing to make amends to them all."*
>
> *"Made direct amends to such people wherever possible, except when to do so would injure them or others."*

These Steps allow the addict to take responsibility for *their part* in relationships and their responses (behavioral choices). It introduces the concept of humility or self-honesty while fostering respect for personal limitations, and the need to engage the assistance of others with more maturity.

The Course Text: Walking with Christ

> *Forgive your brother all appearances, that are but ancient lessons that you taught yourself about the sinfulness in you. Hear but his call for mercy and release from all the fearful images he holds of what he is, and of what you must be. He is afraid to walk with you, and thinks perhaps a bit behind, a bit ahead would be a safer place for him to be. Can you make progress if you think the same, advancing only when he would step back, and falling back when he would go ahead? For so do you forget the journey's goal, which is but to decide to walk with him, so neither leads nor follows. Thus it is a way you go together, not alone. And in this choice is learning's outcome changed, for Christ has been reborn to both of you.*
>
> T-31.II.9:1-7

Step Ten: Alcoholics Anonymous

> *Continued to take personal inventory and when we were wrong promptly admitted it.*

Step Ten creates the freedom to allow for trial and error, growth and change. It teaches a process of development for people that have generally believed in an "all or nothing world." It creates an arena where one can make mistakes and learn from them, thereby reducing the anxiety that is created by idealization and perfectionistic self-criticism.

Step Eleven: Alcoholics Anonymous

> *Sought through prayer and meditation to improve our conscious contact with God as we understood Him, praying only for knowledge of His will for us and the power to carry that out.*

This Step sets the stage for an ongoing relationship of awakening, evaluation, and re-evaluation. This is the nature of mature relationship that gives birth to an alive and healthy psychosocial and spiritual self.

The Course Text: Walking with Christ

Nothing will hurt you in this holy place, to which you come to listen silently and learn the truth of what you really want. No more than this will you be asked to learn. But as you hear it, you will understand you need but come away without the thoughts you did not want, and that were never true.

T-31.II.8:6-8

Step Twelve: Alcoholics Anonymous

Having had a spiritual awakening as the result of these steps, we tried to carry this message to alcoholics, and to practice these principles in all our affairs.

Spiritual maturity is based on a *re-membering* of who we are and why we have created these experiences for the betterment of ourselves and our brothers and sisters. Spiritual maturity is an ongoing process. Alcoholics Anonymous is a demonstration of healing from a disease which permeates global thinking. Actually, the addict is a microcosm of a world in which the desperation of "not enough" and the belief that war and oppression can sustain peace is played out on a daily basis. That one can move from the inner illusion of need and darkness to an inner perception of peace and light creates the potential of this shift to be manifest in world consciousness. Alcoholics Anonymous is built on the understanding that we have choices as we live in the moment (the Holy Instant), because it offers acceptance and boundaries and a support system to identify and deal with emotions. It builds self-esteem based on the positive use of the addict's experience. It fosters development, growth, understanding, empathy, and compassion.

Miracles are the goal of both the Course and Alcoholics Anonymous. Both seek to do this by removing the blocks to the awareness of Love's presence by breaking through the self-defeating illusion of fear. The Course achieves this through its Workbook and Text and AA through its Twelve Steps and Twelve Traditions.

From an AA Member: "I always knew I was a child of God, but I never knew what it was like to be alive, to be a human being, to experience living. With Alcoholics Anonymous as a part of my foundation, I have been able to utilize other tools, other paths which have all led to my ability to be an integrated human being. AA took me by the hand and helped me to trust who I was; helped prepare me to be powerful in the Spirit of which I am a reflection. Through understanding that I am power-*less* in fraud, power-*less* by holding on to what I am not....I can be power-*ful* in communion with myself and those around me."

That we are miracles, divinely inspired by God, is the truth. When we are in harmony with ourselves, we are in harmony with everything around us and everything is possible.

The Course Text: The Healing Example

> *The holy instant is the miracle's abiding place. From there, each one is born into this world as witness to a state of mind that has transcended conflict, and has reached to peace. It carries comfort from the place of peace into the battleground, and demonstrates that war has no effects. For all the hurt that war has sought to bring, the broken bodies and the shattered limbs, the screaming dying and the silent dead, are gently lifted up and comforted.*
>
> **T-27.V.3:1-4**

Rev. Ellyn Kravette is a psycho-spiritual counselor with offices in New York City and the Poconos, PA. She is a licensed social worker, certified addictions counselor, and Ericksonian hypnotherapist. She utilizes an eclectic psycho-spiritual approach in assisting clients to remove obstacles, and reconnect with their sense of personal integrity and potential for living life in the here and now. Her website is www.SpiritualSearch.org and she can be reached at (570) 764-4706.

Chapter 30

Gestalt Psychology

R. Gordon Seeley

Gestalt psychology is a branch of science that studies human perception. Much of the early work was performed in Germany, which accounts for the use of the word "gestalt." In German, "gestalt" means "form, shape, or figure," which are convenient ways to describe certain aspects of perception. Studies show that human perception doesn't work the way most of us believe. In fact, the findings seem so preposterous that Gestalt psychology is one of the few fields of modern science whose findings are routinely rejected. We may agree with it intellectually, but when it comes to everyday living we continue to cling to our old ideas about perception. Perception is undoubtedly the most important aspect of human experience, and yet, hardly anyone accepts the reality of how it works.

Rubin's Vase

A Course in Miracles is the practical application of Gestalt psychology. A simple demonstration reveals the intimate connection between the Course and Gestalt psychology. The well-known image of "Rubin's Vase" where one looks at black and white image where it is difficult to tell if one is looking at two identical faces looking at each other or the outline of a vase.

Rubin's Vase is testimony to the fact that a picture is worth a thousand words. It demonstrates unequivocally the most uncanny, fascinating, and important faculties of the human mind. Even after seeing Rubin's Vase, however, most people continue to believe that the vase and profile images they have seen *are on the paper* they were looking at. In fact, it is almost impossible to convince them that the images aren't on the paper, but *in their mind.* And, our mind is not a camera or a copy machine. If we could look into our mind, we would find nothing that looks like the images we thought we saw on the paper. The truth revealed by Rubin is that human perception is a figment of our imagination! Further, a truth that is even harder to believe is that *everything* we perceive is formed by our mind in the same way.

Ground and Form

Gestalt psychology uses two words when describing a Rubin-like experience: "ground" and "form." The definition of form is obvious, but what is ground? Ground is simply the source from which form arises. In the case of Rubin, the vase and profile are form and the ink pattern on the paper (the source of the images) is ground. An analogy would be a plant (form) arising from the earth (ground). In spiritual terms, ground is usually said to be God or unformed consciousness. So, aside from being source, the other primary characteristic of ground is that it is formless. In Buddhism, it has been called "nothingness." In Trinitarian terms, some would say that "Father" is ground (Source) and "Son" is form (Word). Of course, since form is simply ground-in-form they are, in essence, the same thing, which is probably why Jesus assured us in the Bible that "I and the Father are One" (John 10:30).

The Whole Enchilada

Science further informs us that the gestalt phenomena is active on *all* levels of human perception (auditory, tactile, etc.), not just on the visual level. Combining all levels of perception into one is what produces our integrated view of the world. Since human perception is nearly flawless, we are thoroughly tricked into believing that our view is "the real world." We won't accept that we made it up because "it seems so real." Of course, the Course echoes science in stating that nothing we perceive is real, which, in part, explains why many of us have so much trouble with the Course.
(Space limitations prevent a detailed description of Gestalt psychology and perception theory here; however, the Internet is a wonderful place to search for information about these fascinating subjects.)

Heaven and Hell

Now that we see how Rubin images are formed in our mind and not on paper, and we know that entire worldviews are really gestalt images, let's play a little game...a thought experiment. Recalling from the Course that words are nothing but *"symbols of symbols"* (M-21.1:9), let's change the words of the objects in Rubin's Vase from "vase" and "profile" to "heaven" and "hell" respectively. Now, let's say that whenever we see the white image we are seeing heaven, and when we see the black image we are seeing hell. It may seem a silly exercise, but that is precisely what the Course is trying to help us with...to see heaven rather than hell.

(For accuracy, it should be noted that the Course terms the two primary worldviews "dreams," with our normal dream being hell and our "happy dream" being the equivalent of heaven on earth. Since the real Heaven is a creation of God, it is beyond human perception and, thus, not a gestalt. That explains why we can be brought to Heaven's door, but must leave our perception behind as we enter.)

Worldviews

The preceding exercise brings to light something that is even harder to explain—that it is possible for our mind to organize itself into worldviews. The word "worldview" is useful because it describes the total gestalt we happen to be experiencing at any given time. It is how *we* see the world. We begin making a core worldview as infants and children and add on to it from there, eventually consisting of many diverse parts. Some of the parts are more or less solid and stable while others seem to come and go. Since worldviews are mental formations, it is easy to see that no two individuals have identical worldviews. They can be similar, but are *never* the same. It is also easy to see that worldviews aren't fixed because our perceptions change over time (sometimes very quickly).

Multiple Worldviews

Even more astounding is the fact that our mind is capable of forming multiple worldviews that can be swapped in and out of consciousness just as rapidly as it switches from vase to profile. Most of us have probably experienced this worldview swapping at some point in our own life and wondered what was happening. Now we can see that it is simply Rubin's Vase operating on a larger scale. No one knows exactly how our mind does this amazing trick, but the worldview swapping phenomena has been observed in many people. (Think road-rage for example, or a serious lover's quarrel.)

We Must Be Taught

Another odd thing about human perception is that we must have an idea what a vase and a profile look like *before* we can see them with Rubin's Vase. If we never saw a vase before we looked at Rubin's Vase, we would never see one. It's strange, but we must learn what things look like *before* we can see them. We perceive things because we have learned over time to see them. We all know what our hell worldview looks like because that is what we have been taught and learned. In the same way, if we are going to see a new world, we must first be taught what it looks like. That's the Course's job! It teaches us what we are looking for so we can see it for ourselves.

Varieties of Spiritual Experience

Students of spiritual literature know the gestalt phenomena by different names. Enlightenment, spiritual awakening, rebirth, white-light, and near-death experiences are all gestalt worldview swapping phenomena. All involve a radical shift in consciousness that is no different than the radical shift we see in Rubin's Vase. The form is different, grander, more encompassing, but the mechanism that produces the shift is the same. Since worldviews are far more complex than the image of a vase or a profile, we should not necessarily expect them to form and flip as fast we see in Rubin. However, it can happen quickly, as was the case with St. Paul on the road to Damascus.

And, Switch Back Again

Students of spiritual practices are also well aware of the problem of losing their spiritual worldview—their spiritual gestalt. We can be on the spiritual beam one day and off the next. It's no different than flipping from vase to profile. It happens because we have yet to train our mind to stay fixed on one image—one worldview. Flipping is not a tragedy. It simply means we need more practice in holding our mind on the worldview we want to hold. In time, our mind will respond accordingly. And, yes, it is a choice that we make to stay focused on one or the other.

Conclusion

Of all spiritual literature, perhaps none reflects Gestalt psychology more than *A Course in Miracles.* Once we know what the gestalt phenomena is, it is easy to see references to it embedded throughout the Course. Here are some samples:

> *The world of perception...is based on interpretation, not on facts. It is learned rather than given...unstable in its functioning, and inaccurate in its interpretations. The world we see merely reflects our own internal frame of reference... we look inside first, decide what kind of world we want to see and then project that world outside, making it the truth as we see it.*
>
> T-PREFACE.X.2:1,2,4; XI.2:1,3

> *Nothing I see means anything. I have given everything I see all the meaning it has for me.*
>
> W-P.I.1.H; 2.H

> *It is impossible to see two worlds (simultaneously).*
>
> W-P.I.130.H

> *Yet you must learn the cost of sleeping, and refuse to pay it. Only then will you decide to awaken. And then the real world will spring to your sight.*
>
> *When you want only love you will see nothing else. Nothingness will become invisible, for you at last will have seen truly.*
>
> T-12.VI.5:2-4; VII.8:1; VIII.8:5

> *There is another vision and another Voice in which your freedom lies, waiting but your choice.*
>
> *And if you place your faith in Them, you will perceive another self in you.*
>
> T-21.V.3:1-2

Perception is a choice of what you want yourself to be; the world you want to live in, and the state in which you think your mind will be content and satisfied. It chooses where you think your safety lies, at your decision. It reveals yourself to you as you would have you be.

T-25.I.3:1-3

The Holy Spirit has the power to change the whole foundation of the world you see to something else.

T-25.VII.5:1

Alternatives are in your mind to use, and you can see yourself another way.

T31.VII.6:5

It's no secret that many candidates for *A Course in Miracles* never complete the Course. Surely, it would have been easier for them if they had taken a course in Gestalt psychology before enrolling in the Course. For example, the science of Gestalt psychology assures us that *nothing* we perceive is real…even in the ordinary sense of the word. It also shows us how we literally make up our worldviews from our own experience and project them as though they were real. And best of all, Gestalt psychology assures us that we aren't stuck with *any* view of hell that we may have made. With proper training, we can make a new world and bring it to the forefront of our mind where it will seem real. It may not be Heaven, but it can be the next best thing.

R. Gordon Seeley has been a Course student since 2005. He is retired and lives in Brick, NJ. He can be reached at: Oneness285@yahoo.com.

Section VI

And the Movies…

Chapter 31

Star Wars

Barret Hedeen

What does the Force have in common with Jesus' Love?

There are many types of thought systems (religions, new age ideas, and more) that discuss what is beyond who we are as physical beings. How we interact with this "beyond-ness" is explored by them as well. One of the more popular ideas addressing this in our current mass consciousness is that of "The Force" from the *Star Wars* trilogies. I believe that one of the reasons that the original *Star Wars* trilogy was such a hit is due to some of the truths it shares in its idea of the Force. In this article, I will explore the ways that Jesus' message in *A Course in Miracles* is in harmony with the Force, as well as how it exceeds it. I'll be sticking to the original trilogy—*A New Hope*, *The Empire Strikes Back* and *Return of the Jedi* (Episodes 4, 5 and 6)—for this comparison.

There are several very striking similarities that can be observed between these two thought systems. Both talk about the omnipresence and timelessness of their respective powers. The Course states, *"There is no time, no place, no state where God is absent"* (T:29:I:1:1). In addition, this power is always with us, as stated by Lesson 41, *"God goes with me wherever I go"* (W-p.I.41.h). The Force is described in almost exactly the same way by Obi Wan Kenobi in *A New Hope*, "Remember, the Force will be with you ... always."

Another way the Force aligns with the Course is that both are ways of being that need to be learned. Obi Wan tells Luke that he "must learn the ways of the Force." In addition, much of *The Empire Strikes Back* finds Luke training to be a Jedi with Yoda. In the Course, the path of learning is to live a life of true forgiveness. Its process is one of seeing clearly the instances of guilt we have chosen and allowing the Holy Spirit to undo them for us. This is very much a process of looking within and allowing ourselves to see those ideas and self-images that we have judged unworthy from a place of non-judgment.

Luke's training with Yoda bears a similar theme. At one point, Luke comes upon a cave of darkness and is told that he must go in. Luke asks, "What's in there?" to which Yoda replies, "Only what you take with you." Once inside, Luke encounters Darth Vader, who is one of *Star Wars'* ultimate symbols of hatred and enmity. In anger, Luke slays Darth Vader, only to have it revealed to him that the face under the mask was his own. This imagery points to many key ideas in the Course, one of which is the concept that when we are angry with our brother, we are truly angry with ourselves. *"For you must see him as you see yourself"* (T-26.I.3.8).

Correspondingly, any murderous actions or impulses we have are simply a reflection of our hidden desire to murder God. We do not always see this, which is explored in much more depth in Jesus' explanation of our authority issue, in which we believe we have struck down God, and created ourselves.

> *The issue of authority is really a question of authorship. When you have an authority problem, it is always because you believe you are the author of yourself and project your delusion onto others. You then perceive the situation as one in which others are literally fighting you for your authorship.*
>
> **T-3.VI.8:1-3**

One of the basic principles of ACIM is that *"There is no order of difficulty in miracles"* (T-1.I.1:1). Right at the top of the Text! Jesus goes on to say, *"One is not 'harder' or 'bigger' than another"* (T-1.I.1:2). This core idea gives lie to the part of us that believes in orders of difficulty in letting go of fears. Some grievances certainly seem harder to let go of than others! While in the Course, the idea of forgiveness, aka the miracle, is about releasing attachments to fear, and is an *internal* process, *Star Wars* gives us a classic scene on dispelling the belief in levels from a *physical* perspective.

Yoda is helping Luke start to move rocks with his mind, and suggests to Luke that he can move his X-wing starfighter spaceship from where it is, currently stuck in a swamp. Luke says, "Master, moving stones around is one thing. This is totally different." To which Yoda replies, "No! No different! Only different in your mind. You must unlearn what you have learned." Luke then half-heartedly tries and does not succeed in freeing the ship. "I can't. It's too big," he says. Yoda then says, "Size matters not. Look at me. Judge me by my size, do you? Hmm?" He then proceeds to move the X-wing with his mind, proving to Luke that hierarchies fade away in the face of truth. This scene and this very concept, which is woven all through the Course, evoke the line in the Bible where Jesus says, "With man this is impossible, but with God all things are possible" (Matthew 19:26). There is literally nothing that we can't forgive.

One other way that *Star Wars* and the Course reflect each other is in the idea of a "good side" and a "bad side." In *Star Wars*, the Force is described glowingly, as a universal force that connects all living things. Yoda explains it here: "When you are calm, at peace. Passive. A Jedi uses the Force for knowledge and defense, never for attack." However, this Force has a dark side that must be acknowledged and chosen against. In evaluating whether to take Luke on as a student, Yoda recognizes the qualities of distraction and mindlessness in him, "All his life has he looked away... to the future, to the horizon. Never his mind on where he was. Hmm? What he was doing. Hmph. Adventure. Heh! Excitement. Heh! A Jedi craves not these things." He describes them more to Luke, saying: "Beware of the dark side. Anger... fear... aggression. The dark side of the Force are they. Easily they flow, quick to join you in a fight."

The Course uses different terms to discuss these parts of us. The Holy Spirit represents our choice for right-mindedness. This is our remembrance of love, of peace, of our deepest reality.

> *The stillness and the peace of* now *enfold you in perfect gentleness. Everything is gone except the truth.*
>
> **T-16.VII.6:5-6**

The Course uses the term "ego" to refer to our denial of this reality. It is the belief that something other than oneness is possible. This wrong-minded part of mind, therefore, reflects the characteristics of Truth's supposed opposite. Truth is one, ego is many; truth is whole, ego is broken; honest, duplicitous; joyful, terrified; calm, agitated;

gentle, raging. The list goes on and on.

Really, what we are talking about here is two different states of mind, and we are only always choosing one of them at any moment. *"In this world the only remaining freedom is the freedom of choice; always between two choices or two voices"* (C-1.7:1). Which one do *you* want to hear?

The similarities between the Course and the Force are fairly clear, but so too are the differences, and here are some of the bigger ones. In *Star Wars*, the dark side of the Force is something real and terrifying—you'd best watch out! But Jesus explains to us that however terrifying the ego seems to us, it has absolutely no reality:

> *"Do not let any belief in [error's] realness enter your mind, or you will also believe that you must undo what you have made in order to be forgiven. What has no effect does not exist, and to the Holy Spirit the effects of error are nonexistent. By steadily and consistently cancelling out all its effects, everywhere and in all respects, He teaches that the ego does not exist and proves it.*
>
> **T-9.IV.5:4-6**

In *Star Wars*, like in action flicks everywhere, there is a good side and a bad side, and the good guys had better win, or there'll be hell to pay! If they don't destroy the Death Star in time, another planet will be blown up! Evilness has to be destroyed, and the enemies subdued. However, Jesus gives us a pathway where evil is just a mistaken thought and the idea of enemies is itself uprooted.

> *Innocence is wisdom because it is unaware of evil, and evil does not exist. It is, however, perfectly aware of everything that is true.*
>
> **T-3.I.7:4-5**

> *You cannot be unfairly treated. The belief you are is but another form of the idea you are deprived by someone not yourself. Projection of the cause of sacrifice is at the root of everything perceived to be unfair and not your just deserts. Yet it is you who ask this of yourself, in deep injustice to*

the Son of God. You have no enemy except yourself, and you are enemy indeed to him because you do not know him as yourself.

T-26.X.3:2-6

This is not to say that we don't take action in our lives or do what we can to right the wrongs that show up over and over again in our world. The process of forgiveness is never about *what* we do, but only ever about *how* we do it. Whose hand are we holding as we go about our lives, Holy Spirit's or the ego's? Are we thinking right-minded and peaceful thoughts as we eat, breathe, and work or are rage and tension our allies instead?

Our attitude, as we respond to our resistance to Love's gentle call, helps us to know which track we are on. Are we hard on ourselves when we notice our reactive judgment of a situation? Or do we gently chuckle at ourselves, saying, "There we go again!" When we can choose the gentler route, we are choosing the infinite patience of the Holy Spirit:

One Teacher is in all minds and He teaches the same lesson to all. He always teaches you the inestimable worth of every Son of God, teaching it with infinite patience born of the infinite Love for which He speaks.

T-7.VII.7:2-3

Or, we could say that Holy Spirit is with us as much as Chewbacca is there for Han Solo—always!

Obviously, the Force is ultimately just a plot device that weaves in elements of the burgeoning new age of spirituality here in the western world. We can have fun with it, but it is inevitably outshone by the real, masterful depth with which Jesus takes our hand on the gentle journey Home. Unlike the journey Luke Skywalker takes, to worlds far, far away, we are only ever led on a journey within.

The journey to God is merely the reawakening of the knowledge of where you are always, and what you are forever. It is a journey without distance to a goal that has never changed. Truth can only be experienced. It cannot be described and it cannot be explained. I can make you aware of the conditions of truth, but the experience is of God. Together we can meet its conditions, but truth will dawn upon you of itself.

T-8.VI.9:6-11

I am as God created me.
His Son can suffer nothing. And I ***am*** *His Son.*

T-31.VIII.5:2-4

"May the Force be with you."

LUKE SKYWALKER AND HAN SOLO

Barret Hedeen has been a fan of Luke Skywalker and *Star Wars* since his childhood. As a dedicated Course student, he shares his spiritual journey through his books, *Questions for J—And the Love that He Gave Me* and *Poems for J.* Through his healing modality, The Witness Energy Healing, Barret helps groups and individuals take their next steps on their journey Home within. Visit www.BarretHedeen.com for more information.

Chapter 32

Avatar

Robert J. O'Connor & Cynthia Bove

The movie *Avatar* made a spectacular splash in movie theaters across the nation. One of the numerous reasons that this movie made such an impression is that it keys into the higher consciousness that is beginning to take place in the world. The Course is a philosophy that helps us see the world in a different light, through a different lens. As we work through the Workbook lessons and come to understand who we are and why we are here, we will see the Real World of joy and happiness versus the world of our own making that is comprised of thoughts of sin, guilt, and fear. There are some powerful parallels between this movie and the spiritual philosophy of the Course, not the least of which shows us these two worlds in a very graphic manner. The contrast between these two worlds is exemplified both on a personal level and worldly level, giving us a view of our shadowy ego side and our ability to change our thinking to see and experience our true nature.

To review this futuristic movie, a debilitated ex-marine named Jake is on a space ship heading to a distant planet called Pandora. He is taking part in a scientific project that will "inject" his consciousness into a cloned body of the indigenous people called the Na'vi. The human scientists have developed technology to connect a human's consciousness as they lie in an enclosed chamber to a cloned Na'vi Avatar's body that has been developed in another chamber. Once Jake's consciousness is in the Avatar's body and he infiltrates the Na'vi society, his mission is to persuade the Na'vi to move their settlement elsewhere so that the people of Earth can mine a valuable ore that is only found on this planet and in particularly large concentrations where the Na'vi live. If Jake and his team are not successful in their efforts, the military will forcibly and violently make them leave that area.

Viewers become very much a part of Jake's training among the Na'vi. As time goes by, he learns to respect and become one with his environment. As they slay creatures for food, or the people or animals die from injuries, the people pay homage to the essence that made up that life. An indication of the respect and love they have for life is indicated in a significant phrase, where they say, “I see you,” as if seeing through and beyond form to the true essence of the person. As Jake in his cloned body becomes part of the Na’vi culture, he finds their views, way of life and environment captivating. The people are connected in spirit with animals, plants, and their whole world. They honor their God, they look for spiritual communication and there is a feeling of oneness. It is as if they live in the Garden of Eden. As Jake embraces the Na’vi culture, his final test is to tame a prehistoric-appearing bird, and if the beast is not mastered, it will kill him. Fortunately Jake is able to subjugate and become one with this prehistoric birdlike creature, communicating with it telepathically to have a wonderful flight around Pandora.

This brings up several parallels to the Course, one of which is the ability to tame and overcome that wild and narcissistic ego part of ourselves. Once our ego desires are tamed and let go, our perception of ourselves and the world shifts and we begin to experience what it would feel like to “fly” above the battleground and dwell in the consciousness of the Holy Spirit. Further, we have come to realize when the ego’s thought system is in charge, it is the way of fear and death. As we are made aware of how to overcome the ego by changing our thinking, (taming the bird) our fetters will be loosed and we will be free to soar the heights.

As Jake’s consciousness goes back and forth between his human and Avatar bodies, it becomes difficult for him to see which is the dream and which is reality, showing us the ego in action on a personal level. The Course parallels this idea, stating that we are in a dream state and we haven’t awakened from the dream to find that we are still one with God, and we don’t know which one is true. As we are not bodies, rather as God created us, we are made in His image and, therefore, are not corporal but Spirit. We dwell beyond form as the One Son, eternally unified and joyful. We have only let the woes and cares of life and our environment obscure our true vision.

The Course suggests a way to see beyond the veil, to practice forgiveness of errors that we see in ourselves and our brothers so we can transcend our preconceived notions about form and get in touch with the formless. It is in this quietness that we are transformed out of the ego experience and into our spiritual existence. As Jake moves back and forth between these bodies, it illustrates the struggle between narcissistic, self-involved ego interests on one hand, and embracing our true nature as God's One Son on a spiritual level on the other. As Jake becomes more comfortable in the Avatar body than in his human body, we also hope metaphorically that this will take place in our own spiritual growth, where we are freed from the constraints of the ego and our lives will blossom in the heart of the Holy Spirit. Our goal is to tap into the reality of who we are beyond form. It is here in the world, amid contrasts, that we come to understand we are not different but the same, and that idea will translate into the inevitable thought that what is the same is One. For a time, we will move back and forth between these two worlds until we reside continuously in the Holy Spirit's thought system of Oneness.

The Human and Na'vi viewpoints parallel the two different thought systems of the ego and the Holy Spirit on a worldly level as well. These two worlds are sharply contrasted in this movie, where we see the striking differences between ego-thinking and the more spiritual thinking of the Avatars. The movie reflects the choice to remain in a narcissistic, suffering world driven by greed and self-interest, or the Real World where we can live in the awareness of our divinity, and abide in peaceful harmony with compassion and understanding for others because we have come to the awareness of who we are beyond form.

Certainly there are particular parts of the movie that go the way of Hollywood, and are not the solutions that the Course advocates. For example, the Na'vi's home is destroyed by the human militia, and they attack in turn, creating some quite violent scenes. Nevertheless, we can still draw some parallels. When one sees the human corporation and militia in action, one sees the darker side of humanity, where power and money are sought at whatever cost. There is no consideration or compassion for others and their consciousness is consumed with self-interest and greed. The darkness in this movie is really sharp, deep, and destructive. This is part of what the Course terms the sin, guilt, and fear of the ego thought system and it is depicted here on a world scale. As we endeavor to study the Workbook lessons and become more aware of the ego's habits, we will come to terms with its unreality and then be able to watch it disappear from our consciousness.

In conclusion, *Avatar* has many ideas for us to consider that touch upon the two thought systems of the Course, not the least of which is the differences between the Na'vi and the humans. These contrasts show us two ways to view the world, where before we saw only one that offered no escape. Defense and attack (consistent with the ego thought system) are indeed chosen by humans more often than not. However, now we know we have another choice, to take the hand of the Holy Spirit who knows who we truly are beyond form. He will unerringly guide our footsteps to confirm our partnership with God, and to view all as He does. We are now aware that ego darkness is not a part of our make-up, nor the image in which we are created. The Course reveals a new roadmap that we can follow, where we can rise above all conflict and have the vision that views all creation as One.

Robert J. O'Connor, CSW is a retired Certified Social Worker with forty years in private practice in Holbrook, NY, who now lives in Hutchinson, FL. with his wife of 47 years, Joanne. He is the author of *The Ah-Ha Moments of Life.* He has been a Course student for over thirty years and in the last ten years attended a Course group in Port Jefferson, NY, where he met the co-author of this article, Cynthia Bove. Inkshrink@aol.com

Cynthia Bove is an ACIM student living in Port Jefferson, NY. She is the author of *The Fifth Disciple,* an innovative book that uses the philosophy of *A Course in Miracles* to give a new interpretation to the ancient manuscript of *The Gospel of Thomas.* To find out more, and also read compelling articles about the ACIM thought system, see fifthdisciple.com. CynthiaBoveACIM@gmail.com

This book aims to be the first in a series of writings on *A Course in Miracles* and other similar schools of thought of which there are many—from ancient schools like Gnosticism and Neo-Platonism to 20th century leaders like Joel Goldsmith, Dr. Carl Jung, Thomas Merton and Carlos Castaneda, to contemporary leaders like Eckhart Tolle, Matthew Fox, Thomas Moore or Mooji. If you're interested in any of these topics or have your own suggestion let me know.

jon@miraclesmagazine.org

If you enjoyed this book you might enjoy watching regular monthly presentations by Jon on YouTube.

To enjoy a subscription to *Miracles* magazine please visit: www.miraclesmagazine.org or call: (845) 496-9089

To contact Lorri visit her at: www.lorricoburn.com

Made in United States
North Haven, CT
29 March 2023